Chinese Philosophy

Chinese Philosophy

A Guide to
Personal Excellence and Social Harmony

R. Lekshmi

With a Foreword by
V.N. Seshagiri Rao

shakti
publications
empowering through books

Cataloging in Publication Data — DK

[Courtesy: D.K. Agencies (P) Ltd. <docinfo@dkagencies.com>]

Lekshmi, R. (Ramakrishna), 1972- **author.**
Chinese philosophy : a guide to personal excellence and social harmony / R. Lekshmi ; with a foreword by V.N. Seshagiri Rao.
pages cm
Includes bibliographical references and index.
ISBN 9788194622147

1. Philosophy, Chinese. 2. Self-actualization (Psychology) – Moral and ethical aspects. 3. Harmony (Philosophy) I. Title.

LCC B126.R36 2021 | DDC 181.11 23

ISBN 978-81-946221-4-7
First published in India in 2022

Published by:
Shakti Publications
797/64 (2nd floor), Lekhu Nagar
Tri nagar, Delhi - 110035
Mob.: 9953680097
e-mail: pub.shakti@gmail.com

Distributed by:
D.K. Printworld (P) Ltd.
Regd. office: "Vedaśrī", F-395, Sudarshan Park
(Metro Station: Ramesh Nagar), New Delhi - 110015
Phones: (011) 2545 3975, 2546 6019
e-mail: indology@dkprintworld.com
Website: www.dkprintworld.com

Printed by: Shakti Publications, Delhi

Foreword

IT GIVES me great pleasure to write a Foreword to the well thought out book entitled *Chinese Philosophy: A Guide to Personal Excellence and Social Hormony*, written by Dr R. Lekshmi, Associate Professor of Philosophy, University of Kerala, Kariyavattom, Kerala.

Ancient China has had one of the largest and best civilizations. The present work, which is mainly descriptive, gives yet an analytic account of Chinese philosophy in its historical perspective. It is divided into four chapters, each dealing with a particular branch of Chinese philosophy and the conclusion reached by the writer forming the fourth chapter. Each chapter is concise yet exhaustive.

Chinese philosophy is essentially a treatise of ethics and socio-moral philosophy; attainment of personal excellence and social harmony is its goal. Chinese philosophy elevates the moral fulcrum of people; human relations are its main stimuli. It does not believe in knowledge for knowledge sake; in its view, knowledge should always end up in the cultivation of values leading to immense happiness and social harmony. Becoming human, thus, is its sole concern. The writer's explanation of the essence of Chinese philosophy as the "inner sage and outer king" is really noteworthy and mind-catching.

The three philosophies that dominated China right from the beginning were Confucianism, Daoism and Buddhism.

Confucianism had its sway in China for nearly 2,500 years. In it the word *li* chiefly means propriety; it is propriety of personal excellence and self-articulation. It refers to codes of conduct. Confucianism depicts the excellence of man through another word *ren*. *Ren* means moral quality characteristic of harmony. It represents love, golden rule and ethical wisdom.

Dao means the "way". It emphasizes on the harmony with nature of things. Dao, the founder, was a man of intuitive wandering. The Daoist principles of personal excellence are dealt with by the author in the second chapter. Here and there, debates and argumentations, and analyses that echo are all accommodated in the book.

Buddhism, the third influential philosophy, took its roots in China around 60 BCE. It went hand in hand with Confucianism and Daoism that already existed in China, without an iota of conflict and confrontation. Buddhism is known as an ethicized religion and philosophy. Its message is itself the culture of Asia. The book explains the technical terms as found in the three major philosophies. Mahāyāna Buddhism was overwhelming in China which popularly came to be known as Zen Buddhism.

The treatment of the subject is both historical and synthetic. In the preparation of the book, the writer seems to have freely consulted available material.

The book gives a simple and readable introduction-format to the branches of Chinese philosophy in a concise and succinct form. The book makes an interesting reading as it presents fresh perspectives on a gamut of issues. It fascinates, as it were, scholars and religionists alike. What is important to note is that Lekshmi writes in an absorbing and exciting way.

The book runs smooth with its lucid language. It is coherent, logical and almost adequate. It is immensely deep and widens one's mental vista. It is an important contribution to Chinese philosophy. It has its own insight and inspiration. I congratulate Dr Lekshmi for diligently working on such a project.

Dr V.N. Seshagiri Rao
Professor of Philosophy
Mysore University

Preface

In its profound sense of moral thinking, Chinese philosophy is highly unique. Unlike the other philosophical traditions, Chinese thinking does not capture one with abstract metaphysical concepts or epistemological truths. It is verily pragmatic in its content and approach which finds self and society as symbiotic rather than mutually exclusive. It tends to assume interdependence between entities which applies to relationships among human beings as well as natural environments. The contribution of Chinese thinkers in achieving the sustainable development goals discussed today is worth noticing. The principles and notions embedded in Chinese thinking act as moral proprieties for human excellence and social harmony.

When man searches for ethical principles for a better social living he is to find Chinese philosophical traditions like Confucianism and Daoism acting like the guiding forces. The basic idea of the great seers like Confucius and Laozi is that a human being is a relatively constituted and situated self. Self-cultivation is the ethico-social realization of individuals within their network of relationships. What is important in social living is correlative thinking and resonance, complementary approach to differences, action-guiding nature of judgement and the effective appropriation of naturalness and spontaneity in the interrelations between entities or individuals. The Chinese seers could find that what is needed is not a detached moral individual in a religious pretext but an accomplished moral ruler. The necessity of ethics comes only when an individual seeks not "what I should do" rather "how I should live". Ethical norms must be invariably adapted to the particular contexts of application by individuals which make them relative and pragmatic. The above discussions are undertaken in this work at the backdrop of Chinese philosophical notions like *li*, *ren*, *fa*, *wuwei* and *ziran*.

The study was originally undertaken as part of the University Grants Commission (UGC) minor research project done a couple of years ago. But because of the renewed interest in Chinese ethical concepts and the continuing relevance of the naturalistic tradition of Confucianism and Daoism it is decided to publish the revised work as a book which will act as a prelude to studies in Chinese philosophy.

I am indebted to the Almighty for showering Her grace upon me for the publication of this work. I am extremely thankful to Dr V.N. Seshagiri Rao, Professor of Philosophy, Mysore University who happily agreed to me write a Foreword for the book. This work has come to be a reality only because of the consent received from Shakti Publications, New Delhi for undertaking the publication process. I am grateful to my family members, friends and colleagues who have supported me in bringing out this volume.

Contents

1

Introduction

PHILOSOPHY is culturally at its most visible when it reflects upon ethics and social life. When ways of life contend that we have the stimulus since each needs an ideology, a set of reflections on who we are and what we are doing which justifies the favourable stance. These ideologies or set of reflections must be an authoritative set of tools. Chinese philosophy provides us with such ideologies which, in fact, are an imperative need of our times. It is a moral guide, a moral propriety for personal excellence and social harmony.

Unlike other philosophical systems, which are mostly civilized authorities of reason, Chinese philosophy is, first and foremost, ethical as well as social. In Chinese tradition, doing philosophy is mainly for "the elevation of human minds". It emphasizes human affairs and human relations and has thus the overtones of a "this-worldly philosophy".

Most Chinese philosophic schools have taught the way of what is called the "inner sage and outer king". The philosophers of China have not regarded knowledge as something valuable in itself. But they preferred to apply knowledge to actual conduct that would lead to happiness. The inner sage is a person who has established virtue in himself. The outer king is one who has accomplished great deeds and who brings out social harmony in this world. The highest ideal for a man is to possess at once the virtue of a sage and the accomplishment of a ruler. This is the central axis upon which the Chinese philosophy revolves.

Thinkers like Confucius believed in the radical malleability of the nascent human being through education. For Confucius, humanity is not defined as anything "given"; becoming human is a moral achievement. The formal instrument for personal refinement, personal excellence and self-articulation is *li*, often translated as propriety. Propriety, which includes everything from etiquette to social rules and institutions to the rites of life and death, is the underlying syntax of community. These formal structures reside in the conduct of those members of the community who serve as models of propriety. Such a person could bring his or her life into harmony with the universe as a whole. The implication of this is that we live in a universe that has some sense of order and thus it makes sense to see a way of behaving which reflects order and structure. The chief aim of Daoism, another great school of

Confucius, the founder of Confucianism

Chinese philosophy, is also to help individuals to be aware of and live in a harmonious balance which will promote personal excellence as well as social good.

Chinese thinkers, in general, believe that since personal, familial, communal, political and even cosmic order are all coterminus and mutually entailing, commitment to community far from being self-abnegating is the road to personal fulfilment.

Excellence or virtue (*de*) achieved by members of a community empowers them as likely models of propriety for succeeding generations. Since the authority of community so constructed is internal to it, the community is self-regulating, dependent for its effectiveness upon authoritative leaders rather than the application of external apparatus such as law and punishment.

The chief aim of this study is:

- To bring out the moral significance of Asian philosophies in general and Chinese philosophy in particular. The major objectives include.
- To analyse the moral principles and virtues implied in the teachings of the Chinese thinkers that would help in the promotion of human excellence.
- To understand how integration of personality at the individual levels will contribute to one's good as well as social good.
- To bring out and emphasize the need of inculcating moral proprieties in our lives that may help in the promulgation of a self-regulating community.

- To understand the uniqueness of the moral philosophy in Chinese thinking unleashed against the background of other philosophical traditions, etc.

Historical Background of Chinese Philosophy

Until twentieth century three major traditions dominated Chinese culture. They include Confucianism, Daoism and Buddhism which coexisted for the most part without conflict for over two and a half millennia. They were receiving intellectual and spiritual incentive from each other, thus sharing a range of moral and social values since the time of the Hundred Days' Reform (Wuxu Reform) of 1898. The Western influence was already strong and by 1911 when the Ching dynasty was overthrown by Sun-Yat-Sen, the Republic of China was founded and the three traditions were beginning to confront serious threat. In 1943 Mao Tse-tung established China as a communist State, the People's Republic of China.

Although there are fragments of writings dating from the very early years of the Chou dynasty (1122–249 BCE) the first Chinese philosophers to emerge as individuals were men of sixth and fifth century BCE. The best known of them, Confucius (551–479 BCE) formulated the thoroughly humanistic character of Chinese philosophy and established an enduring system of values that embraced ideals of harmony, wisdom, filial piety and the enactment of rites conducive to ethical conduct.

Confucius and his followers were men of considerable education. They were deeply troubled by the decadence and disorder of the society in which they lived. Confucius did not urge revolution and rebellion but rather argued for a change of heart and mind that would make room for humane government, political stability, a generous education for all and the cultivation of inward virtue and public integrity. The concepts and values espoused were closely related to the daily lives of people. It was directly linked with the guiding principles of social and personal conduct.

Daoism is generally regarded as a balance to Confucianism. It seeks harmony with the nature of things through a quite submission to the Way (Dao) which for Daoists is the ultimate metaphysical principle of being. Confucianism also aspires to have harmony with nature. But it is thought the means of the enactment of carefully prescribed rituals and ceremonies deemed conducive to it. It may be said that the controlled ceremonial of Confucianism acts as a balance to the intuitive wandering of Daoism. The metaphysics of Daoism became the basis of the splendid flowering of Chinese science.

The Chou dynasty, which encompasses the rise of both Confucianism and Daoism, is regarded as the classical or golden age of Chinese philosophy. However, as Chou's political power waned so did its intellectual and social life fragment, first into a phase known as the hundred schools and then into an era called the time of the warring states. Eventually unity was reimposed with the founding of Chin dynasty which was backed by the philosophy of legalism.

Buddhism, the third great philosophic religious movement in China, was founded by Siddhārtha Gautama. It began to take roots in China around 60 BCE, its literature having been transmitted and translated by monks and scholars and its interpretation facilitated by the application to it of

Chinese philosophical concepts. Buddhism steadily gained great support in China and soon became part of a cross-fertilization of ideas with Confucianism and Daoism that was to establish itself as a major religious and cultural influence. The development of Chinese Buddhism known popularly as Zen Buddhism as well as Neo-Confucianism are testimony to these fertile interactions. It was Mahāyāna Buddhism that influenced much of Chinese Buddhism. Among these are Hua Yen, Tien Tai and Pure Land. Of these, Zen Buddhism became most widely known to Western cultures.

The end of the then dynasty brought with it a reaction against Confucianism and a surge of fresh ideas in Daoist thought. Thereafter Buddhism gained in vitality during Taing dynasty with the emergence of the Zen doctrines. Subsequently, Buddhism fell into some disfavour towards the end of the eighth century. A revival of Confucianism was brought about with a remarkable synthesis of the whole gamut of Confucian ideas. Subsequently various versions of Neo-Confucianism ranging from developments of the idealism of Chu His to the critical empiricism of Tai Chan dominated Chinese philosophy until the end of nineteenth century. The interaction of the three great traditions whether combative or cooperative seemed in the long run to result in their mutual survival, regeneration and benefit.

China underwent profound change in the latter part of the nineteenth century. In philosophy the works of Plato, Immanuel Kant, Arthur Schopenhauer, Charles Darwin, Friedrich Nietzsche, J.S. Mill, John Dewey, Henri Bergson and many other intellectuals began to make their impact on the Confucian tradition. With the ascent to power in 1949 of Mao Tse-tung and the adoption of Marxist–Leninist principles, philosophy and politics began to interact in new ways. During the first half of the twentieth century China produced many important philosophers who drew on a wide range of Western doctrines. In the late twentieth century, China's philosophical traditions had many complexities to resolve. Its prime task was to define itself as a scholarly endeavour which is honoured and that too not only in the international community of scholars but also in its own home and in awareness of a tradition that has ever been philosophy as something distinct from the daily lives of people.

The wise words and doctrines attributed to Confucius and his followers formed the moral, social and political structure of Chinese life for 2,500 years (sixth century BCE – 1911). Almost all the institutions of imperial China, its customs, purposes and aspirations were founded on Confucius' conceptions of the virtuous individual and virtuous society.

The Jesuit missionaries had absorbed the Chinese culture and they Latinized the name Kung Fu-tzu to Confucius. Many of the words and thought attributed to Confucius are contained in *Analects*, great hearing *Doctrine of the Mean*, Confucius *Sinarum Philosophus*. These works along with the *Writings of Mencius* constitute the Four Books.

Confucius' philosophy was predominantly a moral and political one. It was founded on the belief that heaven and earth exist in harmony and balanced strength while maintaining a perpetual dynamism. He taught that human beings are sustained by these conditions and must strive to emulate the cosmic model. In the *Doctrine of the Mean* he says:

> This equilibrium is the great root from which grow all the human actions in the world and this harmony is the universal path which they all should pursue. — Chap. 1

Confucius' exhortation to live harmoniously did not mean that an individual's passions and feelings were to be entirely repressed for the sake of maintaining a kind of bland and undisturbed tenor of life. He upholds an imported distinction between harmony and equilibrium.

> Equilibrium is to have no emotion of pleasure and anger, sorrow and joy surging up: But harmony is to have these emotions surging up but all in due time. — Chap. 1

The *Doctrine of the Mean* is the elaboration of the way of harmony. It furnishes the details of the kind of life that, in its recognition of due degree, will be in accordance with the principle of equilibrium, the root of all things. These ideas of harmony, justice and balance in both the cosmos and the individual provided a focus for political theory and practice.

The Major Schools of Chinese Philosophy

The beginnings of Chinese philosophy rested on a climate of widespread patronage of ideas and learning since the time of Chou dynasty. Many of the discussions were focused on morality, political society and good governance. Scholars have adopted the phrase *baijia zhi xue* (hundred schools of learning) to characterize the diversity of ideas and the spirit of debate of the time (Fung 1947: 132). The term *jia* means "group referred to the doctrinal groups" and *xue* means the classifications of the doctrines. The historian Sima

Tan was among the first to categorize the different lines of thought in early China. He simplified their doctrines under six categories (Lai 2008: 4):

1. Yin-Yang school grounded in a belief of two major principles. *Yin* (female) and *yang* (male) and applied in particular to cosmology.
2. Ru school: the school of the literate, and the Confucian scholars were included in this group.
3. Mo school: the Mohist school, a close-knit organization of soldiers and craftsmen with strict discipline founded by Mozi.
4. Ming school: the Mingjia thinkers, categorized in this group, discussed topics relating to the correspondence between languages and reality.
5. Fa school: comprised by the legalists, it emphasized punishments (*fa*) as a primary instrument of social control.
6. Dao De school: comprised by thinkers who emphasized the way (*dao*) and power (*de*) in debates in metaphysics and political and social philosophy.

Salient Features of Chinese Philosophy

Self-Cultivation

The early Chinese thinkers were of the belief that the purpose of learning was to better oneself and society. Self-cultivation (*xiushen*) was their key concept. The Confucians believed that learning and the cultivation of virtue were aspects of the same process. For them, a man of virtue is a person who could legitimately lead the people.

It is true that the belief in the unity of wisdom and virtue has strong Confucian overtones. But the thinkers of the other schools also deliberated on the same. In the Mozi text associated with Mohism there is an entire chapter devoted to *xiushen*. Philosophical Daoism also gives primacy to the tradition of self-cultivation. It involves undoing of many of the effects of socialization and nurturing one's life according to the axioms of non-conditioned action (*wu-wei*) and spontaneity (*ziran*). Yang Zhu promoted the idea of nurturing the self, which included attention to the body and to keep the self unadulterated from corrupting influence in society.

The early Chinese thinkers were of the contention that the pursuit of learning incorporated a sense of morality. This meant that conceptions of morality were often articulated in situational and dynamic terms in order to capture the developmental nature of self-cultivation. It is highly noticeable that discussions of ethics in Chinese philosophy almost always engage with issues at the level of practical application. It may differ from stage to stage or vary from person to person according to ability.

Though Chinese thinking is primarily ethical, it does not mean that there is no place for abstract thinking in it. There was much speculative thought including the contemplation of logical puzzles, metaphors, analogies and suggestive imagery in Chinese thinking. However, less attention was paid to discussions about universal or normative standards and principles. The overwhelming emphasis on experience and practice in discussions of ethics may have instigated Kant's disparaging view of Chinese philosophy.

> Philosophy is not to be found in the whole Orient. ... Their teacher Confucius teaches in his writings nothing outside a moral doctrine designed for the princes and offers examples of former Chinese princes. ... But a concept of virtue and morality never entered the heads of the Chinese. In order to arrive at an idea ... of the good (certain) studies would be required of which the Chinese know nothing.
>
> — Helmuth von Glasenapp, 1954, pp. 105-06, quoted in Julia Ching 1978

The Chinese approval to ethics is not based on a static normative ideal of right or good, i.e. it is not a Kantian sense of "arriving at an idea of the good". Such a concept is inadequate in ethics when looked at from the perspective of self-cultivation. This is because individuals develop their moral capacities at different rates and to different contexts. The early Chinese thinkers recognized that while there are norms of action and behaviour these must invariably be adapted to their contexts of application by particular individuals. For them the basic problem was not to devise norms of standards for action but how these could be applied by different people in different situations. The primary moral question in Chinese philosophy is not what ought I to do but what is the best way to live (Lai 2008: 6).

Understanding the Self-Relationships and Contexts

In Chinese philosophy, an individual is essentially a relationally constituted and situated self. This means that there are many factors that shape the self, which include its relationship with others and its historical, cultural, social and political contexts. Rarely is an individual expected to act as a detached moral agent. According to the general picture of Chinese philosophy, relation and environments largely determine an individual's values, thoughts, beliefs, motivations behaviours and actions.

The above feature embodied in the different philosophers of Chinese thinking can be explained as follows. The pre-Confucian discussions focused on the responsibilities of the ruler. Early Confucian and Mohist debates focused on human relationship in the socio-political context. Later Confucians also discussed the relationship between heaven, earth and humanity. Daoist thinkers booked behind human relationships in their consideration of Dao. The Daoist texts *Dao de Jing* and *Zhuangzi* drew on analogies between the human and natural worlds. In the Han dynasty cosmological thinking which holds that there are connections between the cosmic and human realms was a popular theme expounded by both Confucians and Daoists. During this time, the *Book of Changes* was reinterpreted to reinforce claims about continuities and correspondence in the human, natural and cosmic worlds (Schwartz 1958: 358). Different philosophers share a fundamental picture of life and existence. This is the view that individuals are inextricably relational and are contextually situated. Their central idea is that good relationships are central to good life, as is a stable society within which the individual is negotiable in his relationship with others.

From a philosophical perspective, the concept of self as primarily related to others and embedded in its environment raised concern about the status of the individual. There is some basis for the concern that Chinese philosophy in general tends to focus on collective interests rather than individual interests.

It is better to characterize Chinese philosophy as interdependent between entities or individuals rather than individualistic or collective. There are many discussions about the overlaps between individual interests and common interest reminding us that it is artificial to think solely in terms of either self-interest or servitude to others. This applies to relationship among humans, human relationship with natural entities and the place of humanity in its social and natural environment.

> It is not that Chinese philosophy does not have a conception of individual achievement. Rather an individual's achievements, ingenuity, resource, fullness, as well as malfunctions and deficiencies are only properly understood in light of a person's place in the conditioning environment. — Lai 2008: 8

But this does not mean that the environment takes precedence over individuals, as individuals may alter their contexts. In this way neither the individual nor the whole has primacy over the other.

Conceptions of Harmony

Social harmony and stability were central problems for the early thinkers in China. The thinkers of the "Hundred Schools" deliberated much on the institutions, methods and processes that could endure a more stable and peaceful existence. The Confucian vision of an ideal society sees good relationship as fundamental to social stability. The family was a microcosm of the state, which was guided by the institutions and governed by a benevolent (*jen*) sage king. However, the Mohists disagree with the Confucian vision. They were convinced that the means to achieve harmony was through standards (*fa*). The ultimate commitment for the legalists was to maintain the power of the ruler.

Among the early thinkers, the Daoists stand apart in their hesitancy about social order and uniformity. Nevertheless, harmony remains important in Daoist philosophy. However, unlike the other philosophies it does not hold that the elimination of individual differences is a prerequisite for harmony within the whole. They viewed harmony as a lively interchange between different points of view. In the *Zhuangzi*, there is a particular concern that attempted solutions that do not impose a false unity of multiplicities. It is a truism that Chinese philosophy shows significant features of a holistic point of view. But the whole is not merely the sum of its parts, but it includes individuals, their relationships with others and their place in the whole.

Conceptions of Change

The concept of change is an important theme of early Chinese thinking, which is centred on the theory of gauging or mutual resonance. The notion of mutual resonance crystallizes the concept of interdependent selfhood. It captures the susceptibility of individuals to factors external to their being and beyond their immediate control, as well as their power to affect others. Here the effects of change are viewed in positive terms rather than negative.

The concept of change is very closely linked to that of harmony. Of course, harmony may be thought of in different ways in Chinese philosophies – conformity, unity in purpose, cooperation, integration, order, stability and balance are some of the terms which refer to this. These approaches capture very different pictures of the whole and the dynamics within. In Chinese thinking much effort is placed on understanding mutual influences, connections and change, and how these make impact on harmony. In their view, it is wise to anticipate change and to know how to respond to it optimally in order to attain a beneficial outcome.

The Philosophy of the Yijing (The Book of Changes)

The Book of Changes, as its title implies, attends to the changing situations in life. It teaches, how one must adapt oneself to the changing environments in one's life. In this regard, it embodies the practical orientation of Chinese philosophy.

It is important to discuss some of the major themes embedded in the *Yijing*. This is mainly because these themes are manifest more broadly across the range of Chinese philosophical doctrines and they are constitutive of the distinctive characteristics of Chinese philosophy – (Lai 2008: 11). An awareness of these principles will be advantageous in understanding the moral values embedded in Chinese thinking.

1. *The Primacy of Observation*: The *Yijing* emphasizes observation as a critical element in reflective thinking. Observation helps in understanding connections, movements and transformations in the world. In their deliberations on social, political and ethical life, the thinkers were reaching to the corruption and selfishness in society

2. *A Holistic, All Encompassing Perspective*: The awareness of a larger context is a manifest feature of Chinese philosophy. In the different philosophical doctrines there is attention to the whole, be it human society, heaven and earth, or cosmos. An important manifestation of a holistic perspective is the back of entirely independent or transcendent entities or beings over and above life in the world. However, it tends to think of holism in inclusive terms.
3. *A Dialectical and Complementary Approach to Dualisms*: the *Yijing* sets up complementary opposites in its conceptual framework such as high and low, action and repose, hard and soft. These paired concepts are parts of the explanatory framework of change.
4. *Correlative Thinking and Resonance*: Correlative thinking is the broad view that events and situations in one realm help to explain those in another. In the different verities of Chinese thinking there are correlatives between heaven and earth, on the one hand and the socio-politico realm on the other.
5. *An Interpretative Approach*: Chinese philosophy is averse to working primarily with universally applicable norms or truths. This is not to say that it does not uphold principles or values, but that they are open to interpretations.
6. *Constant Movement*: The early thinkers were aware of constant changes in society brought about by socio-political unrest. They were of the view that the norms

and ideals for the rectification of society had to adapt to the different needs brought about by new situations.

7. *The Action-guiding Nature of the Judgement.* The pragmatic orientation of the *Yijing* is motivated by a desire to formulate course of action that are effective and fruitful. The early thinkers deliberated extensively on topics pertaining to ethics and government in order to improve their situation.

The Method of Chinese Philosophy

Debates and argumentations are the chief methods of Chinese philosophy (Lai 2008: 15). The method of synthesis was a defining feature of philosophy in the Han period.

The study of Chinese philosophy is also critical. Another, prominent feature of Chinese philosophy is its preference for suggestive and evocative imagery, examples, analogies, metaphors and illustrations. The aims of such argumentative devices are illuminations of ideas, exploring their implications and ascertain their applications. The frequent use of suggestive methods provides ample scope for the readers to interpret and analyse the texts. In other words, reading of the classical texts is primarily a reflective activity for the individual reader.

This is not to say that the articulation of theoretical foundations or philosophical truth is not a concern of the *Zhuangzi*. The work entitled *Going Rambling Without a Destination* communicates a belief in the value of reflective activity of contemplation and reflection as an end in itself (*Zhuangzi*, chap. I, tr. Graham 2001: 43). The reflective activity is valued as an end, rather than a means to truth. It generates important questions about the nature of philosophical thinking and the place of philosophy in human life. Not only does it challenge a particular conception of the end of philosophy in terms of truth, it also highlights the centrality of critical reflection in human development.

Every one of us wants to excel in our lives. We live in a world of neck and neck competitions; struggles, stress and strain have become part of modern man's life situations. In his overenthusiasm for satisfying his personal ambitions and achievements, man creates chaos and disharmony in society. We need inspiring ideologies and values that will prepare us for success, suggests ways to recover from setbacks and achieve balanced success and ongoing growth toward personal excellence and societal well-being. It is here that the moral teachings of Chinese philosophy gain importance. They are at once simple but profound ways to a balanced living. They help man to establish virtues within and thus gain personal excellence and accomplish great deeds without bringing out harmony and peaceful coexistence.

Any theoretical study about the making of a human personality and the moulding of a society is interdisciplinary. A study of the nature of human mind, human behaviours and personality development is not purely philosophical but psychological also. Again, understanding social relations and discussing the ways of implementing social order, peace and harmony are political in nature. The rewarding benefits of following the moral Chinese proprieties in achieving stress management and balanced living are therapeutic in approach. It may have tonic effect to those suffering from psychotic and neurotic ailments.

A number of research works have been done in Chinese philosophy. Love of life and living in harmony with nature are the basic dicta of Chinese thinking. This is, of course, the basic dictum of bioethics which is very much discussed and promoted by world organizations like UNO and UNESCO. At the national level also the study of Asian philosophies which for many years never came to mainstream academics is getting more and more prominence in research activities. It is significant and relevant mainly because of its applied nature since the time demands more and more awareness of applied philosophies comparing with other major philosophical trends. Research works in Chinese philosophy are less and hence the hidden but profound teachings of Chinese philosophy for an art of living must be brought into light.

The methodology followed in the preparation of this work is chiefly expository since much of the morals are implicit in the stories and anecdotes of Chinese literature and they have to be interpreted analytically and critically. Some of the teachings have their parallels with psychological theories and some are purely political. Hence, comparative method has also to be employed in undertaking the study.

The whole work is divided into four chapters including introduction. The second chapter is "Chinese Philosophy: A Moral Propriety for Personal Excellence". An attempt is made in it to expose the moral principles underlined in Confucianism and Daoism for achieving total human excellence. The third chapter, "Chinese Philosophy: A Moral Property for Social Harmony", makes an attempt to understand the moral principles implicit in Chinese thinking for achieving social harmony. The fourth chapter is "Conclusion".

2

A Moral Propriety for Personal Excellence

PHILOSOPHERS of both East and West have always discussed about human nature. According to some, human nature by itself is good while for others human nature is selfish and goodness is something which is to be cultivated. Chinese thinking also reflects the same.

In both Confucianism and Daoism, one can find excellent pronouncements regarding human excellence. While Confucianism exposes it through *ren* and *li*, Daoism prefers "naturalness" as the path to excellence.

Confucian Concepts for Personal Excellence

Confucius (Kongzi) proposed the ethical reform of society. He is regarded as the founder of the Ru-jia doctrine. Ruist education consisted in the cultivation of an ethicality which is mainly echoed in *The Analects of Confucius* (Lunyu). The two foundational concepts in Confucianism include *ren* (Humanness) and *li* (behavioural propriety). Together, they crystallize the Confucian ideal of cultivated humanism.

Ren

The term *ren* denotes a moral quality characteristic of humanity. It refers to the primary human virtue of compassion. The meaning of the concept is also revealed in its Chinese character: *ren* (1=) is comprised by two characters, the left signifying humanity and the right, two. This suggests that the concept pertains to human relatedness. Hence, the term has been variously translated into English as benevolence, love, humaneness, humanity, human-heartedness, comparison and sympathy (Lai 2008: 22). (Chan suggests that Confucius was the first to have conceived of *ren* as the general virtue.)

Ren as Love

Ren is to love all humanity (*Analects* 12.22). In *Analects* it is said that only the man of *ren* knows how to like and dislike others. Confucius' idea of undiscriminating love seems to be tempered by his critical assessment of people's moral qualities.

Ren: The Golden Rule

In order to explain the golden rule, Chinese philosophers take the instance of moral person as its starting point because it involves the good and the noble relation between two individuals. It operates on the assumption that there is general agreement between people about desires and interests. In the *Analects*, the concept *shu*, translated as reciprocity or mutuality, captures the essence of the golden rule. In *Analects*, *shu* is accorded fundamental significance in conjunction with another concept, *zhong*. *Zhong* is commonly translated as "conscientiousness" or "doing one's best". A better translation of *zhong* can be commitment or being one's best. To be one's best (*zhong*) – so as to optimize one's achievements – involves the fostering of mutually benefiting relationships (*shu*).

The *Analects* presents a version of the golden rule: "do not do to others what you do not wish to be done to yourself" (12:2, 15:24). In Confucian philosophy, the cultivation of mutually satisfying and beneficial relationships is an integral component of the good life. Self and society are symbiotic rather than mutually exclusive (*Analects* 6:30). The Confucian ideal society is the ideal family writ large: The sage king is the benevolent father of the nation-family (*Analects* 8:6). The family environment is the first context where one learns to put oneself in the other's place.

Ren: The Cultivation of Special Relationships

The cultivation of *ren* begins with the development of family relationships with their correlative emotions and special obligations. In other words, one first learns about human attachment through interaction with family members. Hence, it is said that filial piety (*xiao*) and brotherly respect (*di*) are the roots of *ren* (*Analects* 1:2).

Confucian philosophy takes filial piety and by extension other familial ties as a primary fact of human existence. Within the family context, one learns to be loyal, to empathize, negotiate, love, care, gain sympathy, express regret, balance competing loyalties and priortize obligations (*Analects* 4:18).

Ren as Ethical Wisdom

The *Analects* offers many examples of how *ren* shows itself in the life of the Confucian paradigmatic individual. It is associated with five attitudes: deference, tolerance, making good on one's word, diligence and generosity (*Analects* 17:6). It is one of six desirable qualities of character (together with wisdom making good on one's word, uprightness, courage and resoluteness (*Analects* 17:8). It is realized in different contexts, domestic, public and social. One's commitment to *ren* must be manifested in both word and deed. *Ren* captures the essence of practical wisdom: an ability to learn from others in order to reflect one his/her own situation and to apply these insights to his/her actions. The person of *ren* is confident in his dealings.

The Master said:

> The wise (*zhi*) are not in a quandary; the authoritative (*ren*) are not anxious; the courageous are not timid.
>
> — *Analects* 9:29

The life of the man of *ren* is more a matter of attitude and confidence in his ability to deal with difficult and varying situations.

Li: Behavioural Propriety

The term, *li* refers to the normative codes of conduct in ancient or modern Chinese society. It was a term used to refer to religious rituals or ceremonial behaviours. Yet another usage of *li* as found in *Analects* is behavioural propriety in the ordinary interactions of the common people (*Analects* 2:3).

Standards of behavioural propriety served as guides for correct behaviour in a range of relational contexts: between children and parents, subject and ruler (*Analects* 3:18) and prince and minister (*Analects*

3:19). *Li* mapped out different standards for appropriate behaviour according to one's place in a particular relationship. In this way, individuals are familiarized with the different obligations and emotions that are appropriate in specific relationships. Ideally, continued *li* practice fosters a deeper appreciation of human relationships.

A number of passages in the *Analects* emphasize that *li* must be practised with reverence (3:26, 17:21). In *Analects* 17:11, the practice of both *li* and music is grounded in the sincere intentions and emotions of the giver and the performer respectively. The Master said:

> Surely when one says, "The rites, the rites", it is not enough merely to mean presence of jade and silk. Surely, when one says, "Music music" it is not enough merely to mean "bells and drums". —*Analects*, tr. Lau 1979: 145

Many of the passages in the *Analects* suggest a deep connection between *ren* and *li*; one's concern for human must be expressed intelligibly, in lived contexts. In the words of the scholar Tu Weiming, Confucian self-cultivation is about "learning to be human" (Tu 1968: 51-66).

Ren and Li

Whether *ren* or *li* is more important is a debated question in the *Analects*. Conversations associated with the disciples Ziyou and Zixia emphasize the greater significance of *li* while those involving Zengzi, Aizhang and Janhui show a greater commitment to *ren* (Schwartz 1985: 130-34). This disagreement was later characterized as the *nei-wai* (inner–outer) debate. *Nei* captures the essence of the concept *ren*, it refers to the internal, perhaps, innate moral sense of humanity. By contrast, *wai* captures the spirit of *li*, the externally imposed, socially constructed norms which guide and in some ways limit the inner self. This debate approximates the nature–nurture question within the Western tradition and its implications for moral cultivation. The question that arises here is: whether it is nature or nurture which is more important. *Analects* 6:18 makes it clear that both basic disposition (*zhi*) and refinement (*wen*) are necessary.

The Master said

> When one's basic disposition (*zhi*) overwhelms refinement (*wen*), the person is boorish; when refinement overwhelms one's basic disposition, the person is an officious seer. It is only when one's basic disposition and refinement are in appropriate balance that you have the extremely humane person (*junzi*). — tr. Ames and Rosemont Jr. 1998: 107-08

Ren Is Fundamental

But in *Analects*, there exists the differing views regarding whether ren or li is fundamental.

Analects 3:3 asserts the priority of *ren* over *li*. The Master said:

> What has a person, who is not authoritative (*ren*), got to do with observing ritual propriety (*li*). What has a person, who is not authoritative, to do with the playing of music.
> — Ibid.: 82

The practice of *li* encompasses both performative know-how and the expression of human feeling. Performance (*li*) becomes meaningful only if it is accompanied by the appropriate human sentiment (*ren*). *Ren*, in other words, is the ethical and motivational basis of *li* acts.

In Western ethics, the intentions of the moral agent are often considered more ethically significant than behavioural compliance. Some of the contemporary Confucian scholars put emphasis on *ren*, the inner commitment of the moral agent. Weining is a notable proponent of this view. He argues that commitment to human well-being (which he identifies with *ren*) is the foundation of Confucian ethics. This amounts to show that according to Chinese moral thinking personal excellence means not behavioural excellence but intentional excellence. In cases, where *li* practices are no longer acceptable or detrimental to humanity, *ren* has the role of upholding a commitment to humanity (Tu 1968: 33). In other words, *ren* provides the criteria for assessing *li* practices.

But it does not mean that *li* is least significant from the practical point of view, it is through observing and practising to behaviours that one learns about *ren* (*Analects* 12:1). According to Henry Skaja it is fundamental since it fulfils the spiritual, educative and governing functions. This means that *li* have an educational and civilizing effect on individuals as they instill restraint and observation of propriety. *Li* are the conduit for human feeling, an objectification of the spirit of man. Skaja says:

> Confucians transformed the meaning of *li* from mere "rite" or "ritual sacrifice" to the necessary educative and self-reflective socialization process, whereby man becomes humanized, i.e. socialized. — Antonio 1984: 62-63

If *li* has a basic place in Confucianism then Confucian self-cultivation may be reduced to a socialism process giving no importance for individual development. Perhaps, this is a very common criticism levelled against Confucianism. But educating oneself is first and foremost good to oneself, to the development of one's own personality and then to that of social good.

Ren and Li Are Interdependent Concepts

It is better to say that *ren* and *li* are interdependent concepts. *Ren* is manifest only in *li* practices. *Li* gets meaning only when it is underlined by *ren*. *Ren-li* interdependence has been most clearly articulated by Shun Kwong-loi. According to him, to understand the depth of human feeling is to be able to express it appropriately, one's ability to express human feeling is an indication of one's emotional maturity.

Ren and *li* comprise the core of Confucian philosophy. An in-depth understanding of their interplay reveals many fundamental elements of Confucian thought. The Confucian concept of the interdependent self which sits at the crossroads of *ren* and *li* is crucial to the well-being of both individual and society.

Human Nature

An analysis of the fundamental human nature is one of the prerequisites for an account of human or personal excellence. Whether human nature is originally good or not and what can be done for improving the human nature are, of course, interesting questions.

Mencius of Confucian school

Mencius and Xunzi, thinkers of Confucian school of thought, took contradictory views in the analysis of human nature.

Xunzi, a prominent Confucian Philosopher

Mencius argued that human nature is originally good. Malevolence was due to various extraneous factors that led humans astray from their original nature. For him all humans are potentially perfectible regardless of heredity status. He boldly proclaimed: "The sage and I are of the same kind" (*Books of Mencius* 64: 7). He provides analogies of common human experiences, a liking for good flavours, sounds and sights to support his argument that goodness is also a shared characteristic.

Mencius also attempted to provide a transcendent basis for a moral human nature. He identified it as the source of human goodness and asserted a unity between heaven and humanity. He said:

> For a man to give full realization to his heart (*xin*) is for him to understand his own nature, and a man who knows his own nature will know Heaven (*tian*). By retaining his heart and nurturing his nature, he is serving Heaven.
>
> — *Books of Mencius* 7A:1

Mencius uses the notion of heaven as a transcendent basis of human capacities and potential. For him, *tian* is a source more fundamental than humanity itself; it is the transcendent basis for human goodness. *Xin* in *Mencius Philosophy* is commonly translated as "heart" although the concept covers a set of capacities rather than one organ. The set of capacities is both an intrinsic and a distinctive feature of humanity. It is interesting to find that Mencius did not distinguish deliberative morality from emotion. *Xin* is the seat of intellect, cognition, emotion and affection. It seemed to him profound that the child who appreciated and understood his parents' love would reciprocate that concern and eventually extend it to others. Emotion and moral sensitivity, for him, were, deeply connected with moral deliberation. For Mencius, the task of moral cultivation was to reignite the lost heart–mind. Mencius's moral philosophy stands close to that of David Hume in Western philosophy who also gave importance to feelings and emotions in morality.

Mencius set out four basic manifestations of *xin*:

1. *ren* (sympathy and compassion),
2. *yi* (moral sense or rightness),
3. *li* (respect resulting from recognizing different relations and hierarchies), and
4. *zhi* (wisdom) (Lai 2008: 38).

Mencius believes that *xin* is at the core of humanity. However, what is philosophically significant is whether Mencius "original" goodness is to be understood as an innate disposition toward goodness or the possession of a capacity that may be developed.

The second view holds that humans possess a capacity for developing a sense of goodness. If this capacity is not properly cultivated, it will easily be overcome by the adverse influences in society. Mencius draws an analogy between the nourishment and care that trees should have and the moral cultivation of human nature (*Books of Mencius* 6A:8). A crucial point of the analogy is the necessity of consistent and continual cultivation.

In contrast to Mencius, Xunzi begins with a break, postulation about the lack of moral goodness in human nature. His treatise on xing is entitled, *Xing E*, i.e. human nature is evil.

> Man's nature is evil, goodness is the result of conscious activity. The nature of man is with such feelings of envy and hate. — *Works of Husan Tzu* 157

Xunzi is emphasizing the actively selfish character of *xing* and its antisocial effects. Selfishness results in strife and hatred and creates negative consequences not only for society but for the selfish person himself. For him goodness comes as the result of coordinated social regulation.

The person who has advanced a fair way into the self-cultivation will develop certain inner resources. *Analects* notes that he is a paradigmatic person, *junzi* (man of political and social status and ethical cultivation). The paradigmatic person is a discriminating thinker who critically evaluates the beliefs, norms and practices of a society. He is the creator of standards rather than a follower (*Analects* 2:1, 12:19).

The training required to attain the skills of moral deliberation is extensive. It involves the cultivation of a range of capacities with the following features (Lai 2008: 50)

1. Reading and reflecting to arouse one's sensibilities and sharpen critical skills (*Analects* 17:9).
2. Reflective self-examination (*Analects* 15:6) of one's dealings with others (*Analects* 1:4) as well as a mindful attitude toward all matters (*Analects* 19:6).
3. Observation of the practices and conduct of others. Confucius was a keen observer of other's behaviours (*Analects* 2:10) and he learnt from both the good and the bad (*Analects* 7:22).
4. Commitment to constant practice (*Analects* 19:5) with a view to making manifest one's fundamental principles. This idea is captured in the concept, *xing* often translated as sincerity or trustworthiness. *Xin* is an integral component of self cultivation (*Analects* 1:4-8).

According to David Nivisom, the question of self-cultivation centres on the inculcation of moral sensitivity which he terms *de* (virtue).

Daoist Principles for Personal Excellence

The Chinese believed that there is an ultimate reality which underlies and unifies the multiple things and events we observe. They called this reality the Dao, which originally meant "the way". It is the Way, or process of the Universe, the order of Nature (Capra 2000: 94).

Dao is a difficult concept, arguably the most complex, in Chinese philosophy. It has a wide ranging application in the religious, humanistic and naturalistic domains. *Dao* stands as a metaphysical as well as an ethical concept. *Dao* is reality, it is intricate and comprehensive and, therefore, beyond human understanding. The epistemic feature of *dao*, viz. its unnameability, derives from its metaphysical condition, its namelessness. Charles Fu describes the connection between the indescribable *dao* and what that means for human knowledge: *dao* is ontologically non-differentiated and epistemologically non-differentiable (Lai 2008: 75).

Even as a metaphysical concept, *dao* embodies paradigmatic, action-guiding content. According to Wang Bi, the ways of heaven and earth are action guiding. We are to take lessons from events in the natural world. These lessons articulate the contrast between projects in the human world and spontaneous events in the world of nature. The Daoist concept *ziran* is often translated as nature and used to signify aspects of the natural world. *Ziran* as nature emphasizes a naturalistic perspective. According to this understanding *dao* is more closely aligned with the spontaneous events in the natural world than the artificial contrivances in the human world.

The problem that concerns in the practical action-guide view of *dao* is: how to interpret the term nature. The *Dao de jing* identifies quietude (*jing*) to nature. The *Dao de jing* identifies quietude (*jing*) to softness (*rou*), acquiescence (*ruo*), non-assertiveness (*buzhen*) and simplicity (*pu*).

The way of nature is the way of Dao. When nature is encouraged to thrive and permitted to follow its path without interference it will develop just as it should. Each is uniquely suited to its own life world. People should not try to impose their own design. Instead, they should find the inner pattern and follow it. Artists should paint or draw spontaneously from nature and creative inspiration will follow. The glow of true nature within can brighten the darkness of the unknown.

Chuang-tzu explained the above said Daoist principle with an example of horses. Horses' hoofs allow them to travel over frost and snow and run through the country side. Human beings came along and altered this. They trimmed the horse's mane, shoed their hoofs and placed yokes around their necks. Under such externally imposed patterns, horses are restricted to a narrow path and cannot thrive. These human actions disrupt the natural order of things. Therefore "set yourself free", Chuang-tzu advised (Simpkins 1999: 21).

To be one with nature is, perhaps, the best way for personal excellence. Everyone will prosper if he lives in accordance with nature. All are part of Dao, expressing *dao* by their own individual way of living. Chuang-tzu believed that each person has his or her own gifts and individual talents to express. When people follow this path, nature shows them the way. As problems arise, solutions too emerge.

> Return to your origins in the primitive for wisdom. Problems are only apparent, arising from mistaking relative existence for Absolute Dao. — Ibid.

Daoism expresses the importance of inner freedom in achieving a fuller personality.

One of the famous stories about Chuang-tzu shows how much he valued life and freedom (ibid.: 19). King Wei of Chu heard about Chuang-tzu's ability to express profound concepts with clarity and wit. One day the king sent messengers with gifts to invite Chuang-tzu to his court and offer him the position of prime minister. The messengers found Chuang-tzu quietly fishing. In a proud voice the messenger said: "You have been honoured by our king. He extends to you an invitation to become his minister."

Chuang-tzu continued to fish. Then he smiled and said thoughtfully:

> I am honoured that the king would like to hire me for such an esteemed position as prime minister. But before I give you my answer, let me ask you a question. I have heard that the prince of Chu keeps a sacred tortoise who lived three thousand years carefully enclosed in a chest on the altar. Now I ask you, would that tortoise rather be dead and have his remains viewed and revered in a museum, or do you think he would prefer it to be alive and splashing in the mud?

The messengers could not help but answer, "Of course, the tortoise would rather be alive, playing in the mud."

Chuang-tzu answered, "Then leave me now. I would rather be free to splash in the mud!" Chuang-tzu believed that people will live happy and satisfying lives if they are free to develop. He thought that each individual must be allowed to journey unhindered through the cycles of life.

Philosophers in the East and the West have given great importance to freedom in the life of man. For Swami Vivekananda, freedom is the first condition of growth. Existentialist thinkers such as Jean-Paul Sartre also ascribe greater value to the freedom of man.

Yang Chu, another important Daoist philosopher, also encourages his students to live freely, spontaneously, without conscious interference – according to Dao. When asked what the correct source for life was, Yang Chu answered:

> It is to be found in enjoying life, in freeing ourselves from care. Hence those who are good at enjoying life are not poor, and those who are good at freeing themselves do not become rich.
> — Graham 1967: 141

No principle or rule can be given to guide behaviour. Every rule or principle is one-sided and faulty. Dao is the only possible guide, before rules and words, at peace, the supreme rule. Yang Chu represented freedom from rulers, freedom to be spontaneous, to preserve life, to follow impulse and satisfy oneself rather than live according to sober rules. He believed that it is permitting self-expression and life is fulfilled.

All living creatures have their instinctual way, guiding their unique character and style of living. Ducks live in lakes and ponds, swim and dive under water. Birds prefer to fly. All animals from the smallest insects to the largest whale, if left to live out their lives, without interference, will know how to live and what to do. Each expresses its own nature, thereby living in tune with Dao.

Human beings also have their own individual personality, a function of the way of humanity. People can express their universal humanity by following the Dao. Dao is expressed through each of us in our particular talents and personalities. We turn away from the Dao when we try to go against our nature. Then we struggle. Modern psychology has shown that living genuinely in accordance with one's true personality, makes one feel good. Agreement between one's concepts about oneself and one's deepest feelings about oneself is healthy (Schwartz

1985: 26). Agreeing with the modern psychological views Daoism also holds that if we attune ourselves to the inner being and allowing it to lead us, then our own life force can guide us on life's path.

To the Daoists, essence precedes existence. Without essence, there is no existence. Dao is the ultimate essence, the intrinsic nature from which all existence springs. Empty space, according to Daoism, is not simply nothing, it has the potential for everything. Space leaves openness to be filled. We cannot have a cup without a hollow space. Plato also recognized the importance of empty space.

Emptiness implies the potential for usefulness.

> The spokes of a wheel form around emptiness, the axle. Without it there can be no use of the wheel, it cannot turn. The usefulness of a bowl is in its emptiness. Its essence as a bowl is Dao. Dao is empty (like a bowl). It may be used but its capacity is never exhausted. — *Dao de Jing* 141

We can find the wisdom of Dao when we are silent, quiet and flexible, making space for the Dao to appear.

Daoism exhorts us to return to the empty space, the core of life. Since the centre is actually in the empty space, returning to nothingness restores the natural balance. In restoring the balance, we permit Dao to become manifest. *Yin* and *yang*, the natural polarity of dynamic forces, arise as the inner nature comes into being, in the breath of life, the *chi*. Daoists encourage us to return to the primitive. Living closer to nature in a simple manner reveals our link to the Dao.

The Dao or the essence is there all the time. We do not realize it since we are caught up in the demands of busy routines. Daoism does not reject not realizing or not knowing. Not knowing can return us to the intuitive, closer to the Dao. For Daoism, knowledge is not comprehension. When we centre our actions in Dao, less conflict and effort results. Transformation comes from within, not from without.

The manifestation of Dao in the world is through *yin* and *yang*. They mutually produce each other as polarities that are part of the failure of existence. *Yin* refers to characteristics of softness, passivity, femininity, darkness, valley, the negative, non being. *Yang* refers to characteristics such as hardness, masculinity, brightness, mountain, activity, being.

Yin and *yang* are built into our perceptual processes. The contrast of *yin* and *yang* is absolutely essential in order for us to be able to notice things. We notice differences. There is a good experimental evidence that when we are exposed to sameness, a relatively unchanging stimulus over a span of time, we stop noticing it. For instance, the background noise such as the dull roar of a generator. At first we may be bothered by the noise, but after a while, it goes unnoticed. We do not tend to perceive something unless we have a difference. Sameness leads to an empty perception. Daoism proposes that everything comes into being in relation to its opposite.

Reciprocity is fundamental to understanding of reality. We include this relationship in our understanding of people, things and events. Jean Piaget proposed that mature intellectual functioning requires us to step outside our own perspective and imaginatively into another (Simpkins 1999: 60). Piaget is pointing to what Daoism has long held through the vision of *yin* and *yang*, relationships balance as perception embraces the other's point of view as well. Within the life cycle is a continual interplay of *yin* and *yang*.

Water, one of nature's most life-giving substances, has been used by Daoists to symbolize *Dao*. When water is stirred up, it is murky, but when left undisturbed, impurities settle down to the bottom. The water becomes clear, and all is perfectly reflected in the surface. Likewise, when we are busy doing a lot of things, thoughts are stirred up, things become murky and unclear. If we allow our minds to still everything becomes clear. In perfect stillness we discover *dao*. Chuang-tzu said: "Calm represents the nature of water at its best" (Yutang 1959: 77).

Water conforms to whatever shape contains it, yet water does not change its inner nature. Water can change its state as a liquid, to form solid ice, or even vapourize as steam, without changing its chemical nature. Similarly, *Dao* is formless, and yet it conforms to all things. Like *Dao*, water flows effortlessly, changing its expression according to circumstance, without ever giving up its inner nature. We can find ways to adapt to life's changing situations when we flow with *Dao*.

Water might seem to be soft, yet it has great power. As Lao Tzu (Laozi) explained.

> Nothing in the world can be compared to water for its weak and yielding nature, yet in attacking the hard and the strong, nothing proves better than it.
>
> The weak can overcome the strong and the yielding can overcome the hard: This all the world knows but does not practise.

> Therefore the sage says: He who sustains all the reciprocalities of the country can be the master of the land; he who sustains all the calamities of the country can be the king of the world.
>
> — *Dao de Jing* XLIII

Lao Tzu, an ancient Chinese Philiosopher

Water always tends toward the lowest places. *Dao* also can be found in the lowest places.

> The highest goodness is like water. Water is beneficent to all things but does not contend. It stays in places which others despise. Therefore it is near Dao.
>
> In dwelling, think it a good place to live;
> In feeling the heart deep;
> In friendship, keep on good terms with men
> In words, have confidence
> In ruling, abide by good order,
> In business, take things easy,
> In motion, make use of the opportunity;
> Since there is no contention, there is no blame.
>
> — *Dao de Jing*, VIII

A great message of Daoism for achieving human excellence is contained in the great lines of *Dao de Jing*. It advises us to recognize low as counterpart to high. The logical reason which Daoism finds is that in embracing one side of the *yin-yang*, we permit the other side to form. Both sides are interacting in the unity that is *dao*. Daoists advise people not to seek recognition or public acclaim. Instead, one must act humbly and quietly pursue the development of personal talents. Dao is not fulfilled in external awards or recognition but in accomplishing for itself. Daoists believe that position and honours will come without effort. Therefore, Daoists exhort us to be like water (natural).

Daoism teaches how important it is to follow the ways of nature through the concept of *wu-wei*, the path of non-action. Non-action does not mean that people should literally do nothing at all. Non-action means not to take any action that goes against nature.

> Do not fight against the current, instead flow with it and you will travel a great distance without effort.
>
> — Simpkins 1999: 70

Instead of putting effort into making something happen, we should become aware of what is really occurring.

Non-action depends on a deep faith and trust on natural instincts. Drives and instincts are built in; when left to develop themselves, people tend to actualize their potential.

Modern psychotherapy researches have shown that learning to face with whatever problems one has is more effective than fighting against them. For example, positive results come when people confront phobias. The accepted therapeutic technique is exposure therapy, which guides people in facing their phobias. The same rationale applies to the interpersonal realm. Parents getting into a power struggle with their kids. But a deeper search into the dynamics of the situation will be an effective solution rather than confrontation.

The Daoist concept of *wu-wei* contains a lot of directions in solving many of the problems that man faces in his day-to-day situations. In *Dao de Jing* 135 it is said:

> Plan what is difficult where it is easy; do what is great where it is minute. The hardest things in the world begin with what is minute.

If we take action when a problem is small and easy, we will need to do much less. However, if we wait until things become complex, the task will be much more difficult to accomplish. Much effort is wasted on concerns surrounding action, appearances, getting ready and even what other people think. Otherwise, there will be greater energy for the real objective and success in the outcome. Laozi says:

> When merits are accomplished, it does not lay claim to them. Because it does not lay claim to them, therefore, it does not lose them. — *Dao de Jing* II

The concept of *wu-wei* sounds similar to the *Gītā*'s ideal of *akarma darśana*. There also, *akarma* does not mean rejection of activities but the rejection of egoism in activities.

Yet another concept in Daoism which catches attention among the discussions on human excellence is *te* (*de*). There exists, in fact, an interdependent relationship between the two, *dao* and *te*: *dao* pertains to the whole (reality) while *te* refers to individuals. *Te* is a principle of individualization rather than a general virtue or set of virtues. *Te* is often translated into English as "power". Kaltenmark, Max offers a compelling analysis of *te*. He says:

> *Te* always implies a notion of efficacy and speciality. Every creature possessing a power of any kind, natural or acquired, is said to have *te* (*de*) ...it is an inner potency that favourably influences those close to its possessor, a virtue that is beneficent and life giving. — Kaltenmark, Max 1969: 27-28

Dao is the conditioning context that in part shapes individuals and events. *Te* is that distinctiveness, integrity or excellence of each individual thing that can be realized only in the context of the whole, the *dao*. *Te* comes from remaining in the mental state of *pu*, simplicity. *Te* is *dao*. Inner nature, intuitively followed as a guide, leads to *dao*. By letting be, facilitating others, lead by permitting, standing back to be ahead, potential to influence begins to happen. *Te* means life and the conduct of living power and its influence in life.

Dao and *te* are used in a different sense in Confucianism. For Confucians, the human being, culture and civilization and its rituals are the sources for the guidelines of life. Daoists believe that the source for life's guidelines is always found in *dao*. Personal conduct, family, culture and civilization follow *dao*.

Daoism teaches mankind that how to act comes not from rules, organizations or even culture but from within, in relation to *dao*. Guidelines for action are not defined by external concepts but are found within. If we seek to guide our actions only by an external standard, we fail. Individual situations are a living expression of the greater *dao*.

Whomsoever moulds his person, his life becomes True.
Whomsoever moulds his family, his life becomes complete.

Whomsoever moulds his community, his life will grow.
Whomsoever moulds the world, his life will become broad.

— *Dao de Jing* 57

The best way to express *te* in our lives is to give up the desire for excess. The Daoist view concerning excessive desire is not quite the same as the Buddhists, to whom craving in general is the root of all problems. “No lure is greater than to possess what others want” (*Dao de Jing* 39).

Te is a subtle power, intended as a benevolent one. The Daoist sage guides culture in a peaceful, benevolent direction and everyone fulfils his/her natural potential. When people stop seeking selfish ends and cease feeling overly greedy for paining they no longer seek power and dominance over others. Conflicts and problems diminish of themselves thereby.

There are many areas where Daoism has found application in everyday life. Meditation, eastern medicine, marital arts, art and psychotherapy offer ways to apply the principles of Daoism for a healthier, happier and more energetic life.

Note

Chan suggests that Confucius was the first to have conceived of *ren* as the general virtue.

3

A Moral Propriety for Social Harmony

A DISTINCTIVE feature of Chinese philosophy is that it is at once individualistic and collectivistic. It gives room for personal excellences but not at the expense of social good. It always proclaims social good and social harmony.

Confucian philosophy, no doubt, attends to the contexts of social engagement and focuses on concrete moral practice. The status of *ren* and *li* in the progress of culture and society is worth noticing. The study of *ren* and *li* prompts enquiry into issues associated with the cultivation of the self in a socio-political context.

Li and Te

Whether penal law is required or not for bringing about social harmony is a debatable question in the context of Chinese thinking. In *Analects* 2:3 Confucius rejects penal law (*fa*) as an instrument of cultivation. But Xunzi believed in the positive effects of *fa* since for him human nature is evil.

Xunzi argues against a programme that relies solely on eliciting other regarding behaviour and feelings. He says:

> Now the nature of man is evil. It must depend on teachers and laws (*fa*) to become correct and achieve propriety (*li*) and righteousness (*yi*). The sage-kings of antiquity, knowing that the nature of man is evil, and that it is unbalanced, off the track, incorrect, rebellious, disorderly and undisciplined, created the rules of propriety and righteousness and instituted laws and systems in order to correct man's feelings, transform them and direct them.
>
> — Hsun Tzu 1963: 23

Li encourages positive and altruistic behaviours while *fa*, the system of penal law enforced through punishment, discourages negative behaviours. *Li* and *fa* are complementary instruments for socio-political order (Hsun Tzu 1963). They work in tandem, *li* to encourage altruistic tendencies and *fa* to curb selfish ones.

Li is instrumental in the realization of social harmony as it helps to mark each person's place within networks of relationships. In both *Analects* and the *Book of Mencius*, *li* is primarily aligned with the cultivation of human moral sentiment. But Xunzi links *li* with *fa* and imputes the former with a stronger sense of compliance. This was a major point of departure from Confucius' thinking. Confucius understood *li* and *fa* to be based in fundamentally different conceptions of human good and social development. For him, litigation is only a last resort (*Analects* 12:13). A.C. Graham (1967: 14) expresses Confucius sentiments succinctly:

> Confucius accepts law as belonging to government, but measures success in ruling by how little it is necessary to apply it.

Zhengming

Zhengming in Confucian philosophy is an ethical theory concerning the appropriate conduct of those who bear particular titles. Confucius seems to subscribe to a fundamental normative reality that language terms must correspond with and further propagate. But Xunzi rejects this assumption. He says:

> Names have no intrinsic appropriateness. One agrees to use a certain name and issues an order to that effect, and if the agreement is abided by and becomes a matter of custom, then the name may be said to be appropriate, but if people do not abide by the agreement, then the name ceases to be appropriate. — Hsun Tzu 1963: 22

Li (Appropriate Behaviour) and Fa (Standards and Penal Law)

Xunzi, one of the most scrupulous early Confucian philosophers, argues for the importance of social regulation for the goodness of man. According to him, goodness is the result of coordinated social regulation (Hsun Tzu 1963: 23). He believes that moral cultivation consists essentially in compliance with standards for behaviour such as *li* and *fa*.

Li encourages positive altruistic behaviours, while *fa*, the system of penal law enforced through punishment, discourages negative behaviours. *Li* and *fa* are complementary instruments for socio-political order. They work in tandem, *li* to encourage altruistic tendencies and *fa* to curb selfish ones.

Xunzi meticulously investigates the origin of *li* and its applications. In his view, *li* is instrumental in the realization of social harmony as it helps to mark each person's place within networks of relationships. Homer Dubs, a Chinese intellectual historian, captures the breadth of scope and versatility of Xunzi's *li*:

> *Li* is human emotion expressed, harmonized and beautified so as to become a pattern for all. It uses the features, the voice, food, garments and dwellings, and gives each their appropriate means of expressing emotion. As a pattern, *li* aids those whose expression of sorrow would be too little and those whose expression of sorrow would be too violent alike to reach a golden mean. ... *Li* is the beautifying of man's original nature by means of acquired characteristics which could not be acquired of themselves.
>
> — Dubs, 1966: 146-47

Dub's description of *li* in Zunzi's philosophy captures latter's idea of regulation. This conception of *li* is subtly different from its use both in the *Analects* and the *Book of Mencius*. The *Analects* maintains a connection between *ren* (human feeling) and *li* (its expression) while the *Book of Mencius* unifies *ren* and *li* with moral discrimination and practical wisdom. In both these texts, *li* is primarily aligned with the cultivation of human moral sentiment. But Xunzi links *li* with *fa* and imputes the former with a stronger sense of compliance. This was a major point of departure from Confucius thinking. Confucius understood *li* and *fa* to be based in fundamentally different conceptions of human good and social development. He claimed *fa* to be good at litigation while using it only as a last resort (*Analects* 12:13).

In comparison, Xunzi's approach to moral order and social harmony is more comprehensive and more cautious in its assumptions about human nature. This proposal for external regulation of behaviours appears to be a more viable system as contrasted with that of Mencius' idealistic humanism.

Zhengming: Regulating Society with Prescribed Titles

Zhengming, as its common translation suggests, is "rectification of names". But in Confucian philosophy it is an ethical theory concerning the appropriate conduct of those who bear particular titles. Confucius seems to subscribe to a fundamental normative reality that language terms must correspond with and further propagate. But Xunzi rejects this assumption. He is of the view that the creation of standards through the determination of word meanings is a powerful instrument with which entire population may be swayed and managed.

In their responses to the socio-political unrest, Mencius and Xunzi begin from opposing assumptions. Mencius agreeing with the early Confucians believed in the inherent goodness of man. He optimistically projects that human society will flourish of the inherent sprouts of goodness that are nurtured. On the other hand, Xunzi postulates original selfishness to justify his recommendation for standards and measures such as *li* and *fa* to be enforced.

The early Confucian thinkers were working toward a humanistic government that looked upon the needs of the people as its first priority. Unfortunately, this important theme is often ignored in many popular renditions of Confucianism. The Confucians were devoted to learning and cultivation and committed to optimizing the human condition through socio-political infrastructure. The ideal society was built upon the exemplary and paradigmatic commitment of the government to the people, especially in Mencius' philosophy.

In early Confucian philosophy, the cultivation of the self is primarily a directed process, coordinated by those with moral and political authority. In fact, for Confucius, moral and political capabilities are two integrated aspects of those in government.

In Confucian philosophy, relationships are integral to and constitutive of a person's identity. This concept of self is essentially a related entity that thrives on mutually beneficial relationships. According to this view, self-cultivation is the ethico-social realization of individuals within their networks of relationships.

> The success of Confucian vision relies on the interest of individuals in their shared well-being. The nature of cooperation and collaboration within Confucian society has been likened to musicians playing in a concert. Every member of the ensemble has an important role to play and a good performance is assessed not merely with reference to the ability of each of the players with respect to their roles, but also to how well the musicians play together.
>
> — Lai 2008: 49

The Confucian interdependent self deserves serious consideration as it provides rich insights into the centrality of human interaction and relationships in the lives of individuals.

Mohist Philosophy of Maximizing the Collective Good

Mozi's concern to maximize the collective good is a simple version of utilitarian theory. The welfare of all concerned is the primary driving force of his ethical philosophy. The concept, *jianai*, provides the basic ethical principle for the realization of collective good. Though it is commonly translated as "universal love", it is more profound in its meaning. Graham suggests the meaning, "concern for everyone". While the Confucian relational ethics had its roots in the cultivation of particular attachments, *jianai* expresses the essence of an impartial approach that requires detachment from personal affiliations. It was not that the Confucians were not concerned about social order and collective good. But from Mozi's perspective, their solution was headed in the wrong direction. To focus on cultivating particular relationships as the avenue to realizing collective good would not work (Lai 2008: 60).

This disagreement is most pronounced when Mozi's ideas are contrasted with those of Mencius. Mencius emphasized the centrality of particular human feelings initially in terms of child's affection for its parents.

Confucius and the Problem of Naturalness

An analysis of naturalness shall address three things. First, Confucius' thought clearly reveals the ambiguity of the term "naturalness". Second, Confucius' conception of the most desirable kind of naturalness sheds light on his conception of *li* (propriety). It is relevant to the general problem of moral decision in different cases. Third, Confucius' discussion of naturalness will provide us with a useful approach to the larger question, what is most valuable.

In book I, section 12 of the *Analects*, Confucius' close follower Yu distinguishes between two kinds of naturalness. Sometimes, naturalness is taken as "usages of decorum", i.e. of intricately ritualized polite behaviour. The naturalness, here is, naturalness that participates in this behaviour and is expressed in it. The second kind of naturalness is more closely related to the concept of self-expression. Everyone, even a cultivated Confucian gentleman, has desires and impulses that, if they were expressed freely, would distort human relations and even weaken bonds of civilization. To express such feelings may seem natural. Yet from a Confucian point of view, this naturalness is not permissible. The reasons for this are not entirely social. There is also a danger to the integrity of the individual.

A third sense of naturalness pertains to someone's original tendencies and capacities. To be natural in this sense is to act in accordance with one's original bent, i.e. one's original tendencies or thoughts. It is closely akin to the view of Mencius. He considers *jen* as being present in original nature.

Arguably, Confucius' view lies between these two extremes. He says: "By nature men nearly resemble each other, in practice they grow wide apart" (*Analects* XVII.2). On the other hand, Confucius places great emphasis on training, culture, intelligent discrimination and refinement, qualities that could not be a part of original nature. He points out:

> When nature exceeds training, you have the rustic.

> When training exceeds nature, you have the clerk. It is only when nature and training are proportionally blended that you have the higher type of man. — *Analects* VI: 16

This statement suggests that Confucius' ideal of naturalness is distinct from that of simply following original nature.

However, the Daoist concept of naturalness is distinct from the Confucian one. This includes spontaneity in behaviour, simplicity in social life and harmony with the fundamental tendencies of the universe.

To be natural for Confucius, involves the benefits of education. For him, the art that a good education should impart was more than the art of being a skilled literary man or a skilled government official. It was an art reflected in a pupil's whole character and style of life. As H.G. Creel puts it:

> He considered the study of literature a part, but only a part, of the education of a gentleman. More basic was the cultivation of character. — 1949: 95

It may be said that for Confucius, naturalness that is not permissible would represent falling back to a lower style. The naturalness that Confucius favours represents the thorough assimilation of a higher style of life that is closely related to Confucius' conception of morality. In order to understand this, we have to examine Confucius' conception of *li* (propriety).

The term *li* is discussed in relation to established rules governing ritual behaviour or moral choice. Certainly, *li* is very closely related to rules and traditions. Critics argue that Confucius is basically a conservative figure. However, a case can be made for saying that Confucius' *li* involves much more than simply close reliance on rules and traditions. Creel argues that Confucian *li* involves not only a knowledge of the traditional practices of the society but also "the ability to modify them as circumstances that common sense might require" (Creel 1949: 85). Confucius does not stress the role of learning of an established and precise code of behaviour. He says:

> The honest country man is the spoiler of morals.
>
> — *Analects* XVII.13

Conversely, he prided himself on his flexibility:

> With me there is no inflexible "thou shalt" or "thou shalt not". — *Analects* XVIII.8

In order to understand how we should decide what is right in a difficult case, the following things have to be taken into account. First, an important element in *li* has to be *jen*. The person of true propriety has to be basically benevolent. She or he also has to be impartial and open minded.

> The master was entirely free from four things: he had no preconceptions, no predeterminations, no obduracy and no egoism. — *Analects* IX.4

However, for *jen* impartiality and open-mindedness are not always enough. Some moral problems involve many conflicting prima facie duties. In such cases, well-meaning and impartial people may feel at a loss for a solution. It was for this reason that Confucius considered education and culture relevant to moral development. The education that Confucius provided was not a technical education but it was clearly designed to produce people who gravitate to the right moral solution, to the appropriate action in a difficult situation.

In other words, the person who truly possess *li* is the one who naturally makes the appropriate choice. For Confucius, the manner of performing an action is at least as important as the broadly defined character of the action.

Confucius' naturalness is the key not only to an ideal moral nature but also to an ideal psychological harmony. The ideal person is sincere, having a thorough going harmony among thoughts, words and actions. This harmony among thoughts, words and actions is comparable to the harmony among the works of an accomplished and mature composer.

Confucius considers the value of this higher naturalness to be quite considerable. Furthermore, it has the special feature of being an "inner" value and is thereby much more clearly within the control of the individual who has it than the "outer" values associated with wealth, fame, community standing and love. Thus,

> the noble man is calm and serene, the inferior man is continually worried and anxious. — *Analects* VII.36

Confucius' discussion of naturalness is highly relevant to the problem of moral decision in different cases. The notion that important values can be achieved only by a change of character has not often been explored and it is here that Confucian naturalness draws our attention.

Role of Tradition and Community in the Formation of Personality

To a cultivated concern for humanity in general Mencius uses the term *tui* (push, extend) explicitly to suggest the extension of the scope of human fellow-feeling. He cites the example of King Wan who extended his concern for his family to the common people:

> Treat with reverence due to age the elders in your own family, so that the elders in the families of others shall be similarly treated ... do this and the kingdom may be made to go round in your palm. — *Book of Mencius* 1A:7:12

But Mozi is sceptical about this approach that relies on cultivating concern for others by the extension of one's particular relational attachments. For the Confucians, *ren* is a dynamic concept that denotes specific others (*ren* as compassion). Confucian philosophy regards compassion as the fruition of kinship. While Mozi accepts the instrumentality of compassion in attaining social order, he disagrees that the path to achieve that is through the cultivation of special attachments. In particular, those manifest forms of *ren*, filial piety and brotherly submission teach people to discriminate against non-family. Mozi is not convinced that kinship will successfully develop into compassion. In *Mencius* 3A:5, the Mohist Yizhi notes the implausibility of developing kinship into compassion as well as their basic incompatibility.

According to Mencius, there is really one root of human compassion but for Yizhi, it is two. Mencius' "one root" is *xin*, the mind-heart, while Yizhi's two roots are the mind-heart as well as utility. Mencius contends that the Mohist emphasis on the utility of compassion is wrong because it is detrimental to society or because it is less affective than Confucian kinship in attaining social order. In making this claim, Mencius is subscribing himself to the notion of utility, of what is beneficial or harmful to society. Mozi's consideration of utility forces a critical analysis of Confucian commitments and their approaches to socio-political order.

Mozi sets out a Hobbesian-style hypothetical state of nature wherein a plurality of views precipitates disagreement and hostility between people in the society. He argues that plurality is the primary cause of socio-political unrest. He says:

> Whenever standards differ, there will be opposition.
>
> — Mei 1929: 72

For Mozi, the fundamental cause of unrest is the proliferation of values. He believes that the function of government is to unify and assimilate morality throughout the Empire (Graham 1978: 13). He seeks to replace different values with a single standard that will unify the nation. Mozi refers to the unifying code as a standard, *fa*. The concept of *fa* in early Chinese philosophy has a range of meanings including normative standard or principle, a model or instance of the standard or even a paradigmatic person who realizes it. In Mohist philosophy, *fa* has a pragmatic aspect and is most often used to refer to a model or paradigm.

The paradigmatic person in Mohist philosophy realizes different instantiations of rightness, *yi*. Instantiations of *yi* are beneficial (benefit, utility: *li*). When people are united in their commitment to social utility, clarity of right and wrong is achieved. The wise ruler determines standards of right (*shi*) and wrong (*fa*) and the common people are to follow them.

Mozi is of the view that the common people are not expected to engage in or contribute to decisions about the standards. The common people are responsible for maintaining these standards. They are required to inform the appropriate higher level authority about the exemplary instantiations of standards or breaches of it.

But the denial of the common people's ability to make independent judgements and the reliance on external motivation for ethical behaviour are incompatible with contemporary liberal notions of selfhood and citizenship. Mozi justifies his totalitarian impositions by anchoring the standard in heaven's intention. The authority for the standard lies in a transcendent source, even beyond the decisions of the emperor. At times, Mozi takes a more humanistic approach and appeals to the concern of heaven for all humanity.

It appears that Mozi's primary concern is not to specify the nature of heaven but to present on ultimate authority for the standard *yi*. Because heaven desires *yi*, humans by implication should also. Mozi said:

> Be obedient. Be careful. Be sure to do what Heaven desires and avoid what Heaven abstains from. — Tr. Mei 1929: 151

The rationale for *yi* (righteousness) as the standard is its efficacy in bringing about good order.

> When there is righteousness in the world, then the world is well ordered, but when there is no righteousness then it is in disorder. — Watson 1999: 74

In brief, *yi* is valued as a means to an end; it helps in the realization of socio-political order. Heaven is the paradigmatic *fa*, the agent that realizes *yi*. For humans to keep to the standard is to adopt heaven's perspective of impartiality.

There are three criteria (*san fa*) according to which all assertions, practices and actions must be assessed. They are precedent, empirical veracity and utility.

a. Precedent	Mozi frequently discusses the actions of previous sage kings and the outcomes of their actions.
b. Empirical veracity	The saying or action is checked against the experiences of the common people.
c. Utility	This is the most important consideration for Mozi. He was rejecting the appeals to tradition and authority that were common argumentation strategies in early Chinese philosophy.

The three criteria constitute the underlying argumentation structure of Mozi's entire philosophy. The process of measuring aids one's discrimination (*bian*) between what is useful and what is not. The different areas of enquiry for Mozi – ranging from the ethical to the technical – require the same methods of verification. His epistemology is simple and undifferentiated and one between the different types of knowledge – as indeed he compares heaven's will with the compass of the wheelwright and the square of the carpenter (Lai 2008: 68).

These analogies reflect Mozi's concept of ethical deliberation. His picture of humanity is very much reduced from the Confucian vision of moral cultivation and self-development. It appears that Mozi has extrapolated moral reasoning from craftsmanship. The major implication of this is that morality becomes a skill of recognizing patterns and fitting the same. Accordingly, the Mohist conception of knowledge is not about the accumulation of information but the practical applications of things and ideas. To know something is to be able to distinguish it – to pick it out – from others (*bian*). Mozi resorts to *bian* (distinguishing) to resolve the problems of *bian* (disagreements) (Lai 2008: 68). The concept of *bian* (distinguish) captures the essence of Mohist epistemology. In this respect, to know is to have a skill to make distinctions.

Wu-wei and Government

The Daoist concept of *wu-wei* (no action) is often associated with a Daoist style of government and leadership. It can be understood in a range of ways in relation to government. It may be understood to refer to the style of government, its organizational structures, its objectives and more broadly, its view of human life in society. It derides conventional markers of success including social status, wealth and economic inequality as these produce conflict, disorder, envy and crime (*Dao de Jing* 3.4).

At the most fundamental level, *wu-wei* involves the rejection of a government style or institution that oppresses the people and threatens them (*Dao de Jing* 30.31). Its resentment of corruption is also palpable (*Dao de Jing* 53.75). *Wu-wei* may also be understood in terms of a government that does not impose unnecessary restrictions on the people (*Dao de Jing* 57.58) or one that does not resort to the wrong kinds of measures, such as the promotion of sagehood (*Dao de Jing* 18.19). One can detect in this work themes that are consonant with a liberal democratic conception of society. For instance, the Daoist sage has no fixed (personal) ideas ... he regards the people's ideas as his own (*Dao de Jing* 49).

The *Dao de Jing* criticizes the then contemporary institutions because their intrusiveness and excessive regulation are symptomatic of a lack of trust in the common people.

> It is only when (the ruler) does not have enough faith in others that others will have no faith in him. — *Dao de Jing* 17

It appears to advocate equality among the people, especially in its contrast between the way of heaven and the way of humanity. It is said:

> *Heaven's way is indeed the bending of a bow*
> *When high, bring it down*
> *When it is low, raise it up*
> *When it is excessive, reduce it*
> *When it is insufficient, supplement it.*
> *The way of Heaven reduces whatever is excessive and supplements whatever is insufficient.*
> *The way of man is different.*
> *It reduces the insufficient to offer to the excessive.*
>
> — *Dao de Jing* 77

These views of government seem to reflect not only disenchantment with the existing institutions. They are also deeply suspicious of the assumptions about human nature that were correlated with and which justified the use of these institutions. The understanding of *wu-wei* appears reasonable and appealing in the contemporary context, if we can supply a substantive account of the socio-political goods that the Daoist sage is to promote. *Wu-wei* can generate a number of different models of political leadership. *Wu-wei* may be employed in political ideology in order to restrict the freedoms of the common people.

The following lines seems to express the view of government that keeps the people simple.

> *Therefore in the government of the sage,*
> *He keeps their hearts vacuous,*
> *Fills their bellies,*
> *Weakens their ambitions — Dao de Jing*, tr. Chan, 103

This passage may be understood to advocate a manipulative political strategy. However, most scholars have tried to defend the notion of vacuity in terms of a simpler, unadulterated lifestyle. But one cannot simply brush aside the interpretation of *wu-wei* as a dictate to submit to the greater socio-political order (Graham 1967: 289). A *wu-wei* government in this case is one according to which the people are to go with the flow; to submit to the administration of the government.

Shen Dao, a legalist thinker who had influenced both Daoism and Legalism, was said to have let other things carry him along (Ibid.: 279). According to Schwartz, this suggests a call for submission to the dynamic forces of the larger socio-political order (Schwartz 1985: 244). Here one can see the ambiguities of *wu-wei*. It can be drawn upon to support drastically different models of government.

The Ethics of Ziran and Wu-wei

The *Dao de Jing* aligns a set of metaphors associated with submissiveness and inferiority. In this context, it is better to throw some light on *ziran*, which is often translated as "nature", to designate entities in the natural world and the relations between them. The ethical system derived from this conception of *ziran* models itself on the ways of nature. It is one that defies human control and embodies "spontaneous patterns, routines, cycles, rhythms and habits" (Schwartz 1958: 202). The ethical response corresponding to a world of this sort is *wu-wei*, non-interference or telling things to. This is how Chan understands the paradigmatic ethic of the Daoist sage and he supports all things in their natural (*ziran*) state but does not take any action (*wu-wei*) (*Dao de Jing* 64).

Xiaogan Liu, a contemporary Daoist scholar, identifies *ziran* as the core value in Daoist ethics (Lai 2008: 105). He argues that this is a system in which interpersonal relationships are characterized by naturalness and peace and that, ultimately, the ethic is reducible to the basic relationship between the people and naturalness.

> Although earth, heaven, and the way are very important concepts in Laozi's philosophy they are only transitional or intermediate concepts. They are necessary for expository and rhetorical purposes, but the emphasis really lies on the two ends of the spectrum - people and naturalness - and the relationship between these two. What this reveals is that people - and particularly the ruler - should emulate naturalness. — Lai 2008: 220-21

But a shortcoming of an appeal to the ethic of naturalness is that it fails to illuminate what it is about naturalness that should be emulated. There and it is not clear which characteristics we should follow. Lin's account assumes that there is an agreed, predetermined conception of naturalness and that life must be conducted according to its specifications.

However, there is another interpretation of *ziran*. As an adjective, *ziran* designates spontaneity – the way the entity is what is so of itself (Waley 1942: 174). This understanding of *ziran* does not appeal to the natural world. Instead, it is grounded in a Daoist notion of self; one that is free to articulate itself within its environing conditions.

The two interpretations of *ziran* as nature and spontaneity seem to have opposite implications. To be *ziran* (natural) is to follow a prescribed path of development, that which is natural. To be *ziran* (spontaneous) is to be free from undue coercion:

> One important aspect of *tzu-jan* (*ziran*) is that the movement of things are spontaneous and never results from engineering or conditioning by an external power.
>
> — Cheng 1977: 356

The differences between the two interpretations of *ziran* are particularly pronounced when we consider the thesis in *Dao de Jing* in terms of the natural world.

> *Man models himself after Earth*
> *Earth models itself after Heaven*
> *Heaven models itself after Dao*
> *And* Dao *models itself after Nature. — Dao de Jing* 25

And in terms of spontaneity;
Humans emulate earth
Earth emulates Heaven
Heaven emulates Dao
Dao emulates spontaneity.

What is at the core of *ziran* as spontaneity is a principle or a characteristic rather than an entity or organism (the natural world). Spontaneity in the Daoist senses does not mean unfettered freedom. The idea of *ziran* as "self-so" is not a philosophy promoting complete self-determination. Instead, it should be understood as a concept that incorporates the fundamental relationality of entities and their embeddedness in their contextual environments. In this way, it is not difficult to see how spontaneity can apply both to individuals as well as the states of affairs. In relation to the latter, it denotes the relationships between entities, the effects they have on each other and their continuing mutual transformation.

If we accept this analysis of *ziran*, we can also understand *wu-wei* as an appreciation of the spontaneity (of the other) (Lai 2008: 107). Within a framework that views individuals as interdependent, recognition of the other's spontaneity, distinctness and separateness entails an ethical response of non-interference, *wu-wei*. Non-interference has many significant ethical implications. These include an avoidance of inflexible, absolutist ideals and unilateral and dictatorial methodologies as well as promotion of those that engender a measure of individual self-determination. *Ziran-wu-wei* describes an ethical framework that is grounded in respect for individual spontaneity. It seems that one may not assume that the practice of *ziran-wu-wei* is natural to humanity and therefore comes easily. In fact, it needs a deep wisdom coupled with particular skills. The most explicit articulation of the *ziran-wu-wei* ethic can be found in the *Dao de Jing.*

> He who takes conventionally prescribed action (*wei*) fails. Therefore, the sage takes (*wei*) unconditioned and non-controlling action (*wu-wei*) and therefore does not fail.

> He seeks not to control anything and therefore he does not lose anything. He learns to be divested of conventional norms and their associated conditioned perspectives (*xue burue*). And returns to the original multiplicity and specificity (of individuals). Thus he supports all to be spontaneous and not to act according to learned and continued responses (*Dao de Jing* 64).

Shu: The Technique of Managing the Bureaucracy

In the context of the legalist philosophy of China, one can find a unique technique of managing the bureaucracy.

Shen Buhai was a successful minister of Han Fei, who is regarded as the synthesizer of legalist philosophy. He discussed the political techniques that would lead to the desired outcome, not through reverting to the assertion of kingly power but in the installation of a system that could objectively measure the abilities and achievements of the officials. His plan was to establish a system of mechanism to limit the powers of officials. In this way, Shen's ruler resembles Hobbes' ruler who is the guardian of the social contract but who alone is not subject to its statutes. His ideas sound modern in the sense that they have moved away from reliance on interpersonal relationships and patrimonial bureaucracy to the establishments of institutional infrastructure (Lai 2008: 178).

According to Shen, the ruler is dependent on the expertise of his advertisers. But to admit or reveal his dependence is dangerous. The ruler's position is a deeply alienating one in the sense that it is essentially dependent on the bureaucrats but requires a face of independence and superiority. Han fei identifies Shen's core concept as *shu*, the technique. In fact, *shu*, the ruler's technique is secret.

Yet, in large part, *shu* is not concealed as it is enforced in the system of fixing names (*xing ming*). This theory focuses on the definition of specific tasks and responsibilities that relate to particular offices, that is, the designated titles of the functionaries must be properly matched to their responsibilities. This is, in fact, not entirely new. The Confucians advocated the normative imposition of titles (*zhanming*). Xunzi emphasized the power of the ruler in devising and imposing standards of behaviour through titles.

Some of the views held by Shen Buhai incorporate references to Daoist *wu-wei*. There are passages which make the Legalist Daoist ruler benevolent.

The ruler is like a mirror, which merely reflects the light that comes to it, itself doing nothing, and yet, because of its mere presence, beauty and ugliness present themselves to view. ... The ruler's method is that of complete acquiescence. He merges his personal concerns with the public good, so that as an individual he does not act. He does not act, yet as a result of his new action (*wu-wei*) the world brings itself to a state of complete order (Shun 1997: 63-64).

Han Fei argues somewhat in Confucian terms that virtuous leadership is more fundamental than political power. He maintains the importance of authority but points out that it is derivative and not fundamental. He also considered Daoist ideas, commenting extensively on a number of passages from the *Dao de Jing*. For instance, where the *Dao de Jing* draws an analogy between governing a nation and cooking fish – and the first is not to be turned over too often – Han Fei argues that the metaphor instructs the ruler not to change laws too frequently (Watson 1963: 185).

The ruler's power against the people was sustained by the use of objective, clearly-promulgated penal laws. This strategy was to be kept secret. The ruler's power is most secure when *fa* is publicized as widely as possible, while strategy, *shu*, was kept as a closely guarded secret. Shang Yang and Shen Buhai share in the condition that secrecy is integral to political power. Han Fei articulated the inverse proportions between publicity (of *fa*) and secrecy (of *shu*).

Democratic Principles in Chinese Philosophy

In today's world we urgently need to think well about whether democracy is, or is not, alien to non-Western traditions. We also need to ask whether if the idea of democracy is in some sense alien, this should be thought to matter at all for normative and political purposes.

Democracy, broadly speaking, means rule by the people. It is a form of decision making or a form of government. Philosophical accounts of democracy analyse its nature and discuss its value. The concept of democracy may naturally be thought of as what G.B. Gallie called an essentially contested concept. Such concepts are those whose analysis is irresolvable because different analysts read into it their favoured values.

Confucianism had a very definite and well-defined system of moral and social philosophy. To the Chinese it is contained in one word, *li* which has a broad sense. In the narrowest sense it means propriety and good manners. It subjects the political order to the moral social order, making the latter the basis of the former. Confucianism implies a naive trust in the rulers almost as naive as the idea that a true government by the demos has ever become a reality. The people got to learn to regulate their lives socially and not rely upon the law.

Regarding the moral ideal of government, Confucius said:

> Guide the people with governmental measures and control or regulate them ... but will have no sense of honour or shame. Guide the people by virtue and control or regulate them by *li* and people will have a sense of honour and respect.
> — Yutang 1959: 266

The Confucian ideal political community is of each person exercising moral self-scrutiny and self-cultivation. Education of others and continuing self-education are important ideals. Persuasion and non-violent moral examples are preferred to the use of free and harsh legalism. Hence, democracy is not far away as an ideal. There is some pragmatic value in making democracy seem continuous with a powerful self-conception.

Francis Fukuyama accentuates the aspects of Confucianism that support democracy, emphasizing the value it sets on education which in modernization theory is viewed as supportive of democracy. Education brings about a turn from economic thinking to political thinking and the associated desire to participate in political decision making.

In his books and articles on Political Confucianism, Jiang Qing calls for a restoration of Confucianism as the state ideology. He outlines a Confucian political structure strongly distinct from both Soviet style communism and Western style democracy. He points out that the Western style democratic system if applied to China would have only one legitimacy, popular will or civil legitimacy. Such unilegitimacy operates only on the quality of voters, regardless of the moral implications of the decisions taken. Since human desire is selfish those decisions can be self-serving for a particular majority's interest.

In contrast the Confucian state which Jiang proposes is tri-legitimate; it carries numinous historical and civil legitimacy simultaneously. In particular the governmental body consists of three mutually constraining institutions that represent religion, cultural tradition and popular will.

The abovesaid ideas can be traced back to a Confucian concept. "The sovereign rules through the heaven, the earth and the people" (*Analects* XV.4). Jiang believes that such a structure would avoid many of the mistakes that appear inevitable under a unilegitimate system.

Mencius had contributed a great deal to the ideal of democracy. His definite contributions to the democratic principle are as follows. First, that all men are equal. Second, of the three elements of a state, the people are the most important and the ruler is the least important. Third, decisions of promotion and punishment are to be based not on what the government officials say but on what the people say. Fourth, government must be for the welfare of the people and the king must share his pleasures with the people. Fifth, the relationships of the ruler and the people are reciprocal. Sixth, the right to revolt was vindicated. Finally, Mencius constantly elaborated the idea in the *Book of History* that the emperor ruled his country as a mandate from the heaven and forfeited it as soon as he misruled. Ultimately anyone rules only because the people accept him. Regarding the different elements of a state, he said:

> The people are the most important, the spirits of the state second and the ruler the last important of all.
>
> — Yutang 1959: 178-79

In his view all men can be Yao and Shun, i.e. ideal sage emperors.

From his general idealism Mencius developed the theory of "benevolent government" which became the keystone of Chinese political philosophy. He also developed the distinction between "the royal way" and "the dictators way" or government by winning the people's hearts and government by force.

Mencius gives the following instructions for a democratic ruler. An intelligent ruler, in his view, will regulate the livelihood of the people, so as to make sure that they shall have sufficient wherewith to support their wives and children, that in good years they shall always be abundantly satisfied and that in bad years they shall not be in danger of perishing.

Motse, the indigenous religious teacher of China, taught universal love as the basis of society and of peace. Some of his messages are essentially democratic in approach. He said:

> The interest of the wise ruler lies in carrying out what makes for order among the people and avoiding what makes for confusion. — Yutang 1959: 221

In his view, when the administration of the ruler answers to the desires of the subjects there will be order, otherwise there will be confusion. When the administration of the ruler answers to the desires of the subjects it manifests an understanding of the approvals and disapprovals of the people.

Motse found the secret of good democratic practice in universal love and mutual aid. In his view, when the ruler and the ruled love each other, they will be gracious and loyal, when father and son love each other they will be affectionate and filial, when the elder and the younger brothers love each other they will be harmonious.

> When all the people in the world love one another then the strong will not overpower the weak, the many will not apprise the few, the wealthy will not mock the poor, the honoured will not disdain the humble and the cunning will not deceive the simple. And it is all due to natural love that calamities, strifes, complaints and hatred are prevented from arising. Therefore, the benevolent exalt it.
>
> — Yutang 1959: 226

Mao Tse-tung understood the term, democracy to mean letting people speak out on topic about which they have some direct knowledge. The people have useful concrete information that can help official make good policies. Letting them speak out also helped to unify the party and the people, it promotes cohesiveness. Thus democracy is a useful tool for leaders to employ.

For the Chinese Marxists, the expression, "mass line practice" embodied democracy. It arose during the guerilla period to refer to the custom of consulting with local people or carrying out local investigations prior to expanding operations to a larger area where that locally derived information would be applicable.

A striking feature of modern Chinese philosophy is its retrieval of the traditional Chinese thinking as a resource for addressing twentieth-century concerns. Many of the

Mao Tse-tung, the founding father of
People's Republic of China

above-discussed democratic principles need to be applied and practised in the modern democratic set-up today.

In the contemporary times what we call "liberal democracy" is enclosed by almost all people. Today, democracy as a political regime more or less identified with free individual choice, i.e. liberal democracy. But at the same time it also meets severe criticisms which include negative and positive liberty. During the important phases of Western political development liberal democracy has been criticized by able thinkers. On a philosophical plane, the most important development was the pragmatism of John Dewey. For Dewey,

> democracy as an ideal for community life is not a mere provision for a minimal state which simply leaves citizens alone. The clear consciousness of a communal life in all its implications constitutes the idea of democracy.
>
> — Boisvert 1998: 51-52

In recent times many of the Western political theorists have come for a reconnection of ethics and politics. What is needed today is a new understanding of democracy in the sense of a transformative popular self rule. In other words, democracy is to be understood as a broad human ideal as the ancient Chinese thinkers held in high esteem. The need for a rethinking of traditional teachings is today acknowledged by many Neo-Confucians such as Tu Weiming and Liu Shu-hscim. Taking Chinese wisdom in the direction of a responsible democratic ethos, China scholar Henry Rosemont Jr. in his *A Chinese Mirror* observes that democracy might be described as a regime in which every member has the right and duty to participate in public affairs and to take the public welfare of all the other members of society as one's own. In other words, democracy involves a striving toward human flourishing on both individual and social levels if it is to realize its true ideal.

The principles and practices needed for an ideal social order found through Chinese thinking are highly relevant in the modern context.

Note

The concept of human nature discussed Mencius and Xunzi sounds similar to that of Hobbes and Locke in the Western thought.

4

Conclusion

CHINESE thinking is highly philosophical because of its reflective nature and is unique for its own method and style. The early Chinese thinkers, in different contexts, engaged in systematic, reflective enquiry. They considered ethical questions, meta-ethical issues, the nature of man, the nature of government, metaphysical visions, the role of language as well as argumentation, all of which are core philosophical activities.

In fact, the distinctive features of Chinese philosophy are spread across many of the distinguished themes of traditional Western philosophy: ethics and political philosophy, metaphysics, epistemology and logic. However, the dominant paradigms in Chinese and Western philosophy which include the conception of the self, common good, existence, causality, language and its relation with reality, knowledge and wisdom are not always similar in their approaches.

Chinese philosophy presents a dynamic and realistic picture of the self at the centre of ethical discussions. The conceptions of the self in Chinese philosophy as a relationally constituted and culturally, historically situated person are complicated and profound.

The method of Chinese philosophy is unique. It is unique in the sense that it is mostly for synthesis rather than analysis as we find in most of the Western philosophical traditions. Perhaps, in being exposed to many different views, the early Chinese thinkers could see the merits in the views of other doctrines. The production of different views may have engendered in the Chinese thinkers a disposition toward compromise and synthesis rather than analysis and definition. In broad terms, the method of synthesis looks for concordances and is comfortable with drawing elements from different, sometimes incompatible doctrines. The analytic approach, by contrast, seeks to understand the constitutive elements of each doctrine as well as how these are combined in argumentation. This approach also focuses on systematization, which the Chinese intellectual traditions seemed to lack. However, the method of synthesis, which continues to be a dominant method in scholarship in modern-day China appreciates different perspectives and pragmatically seeks to draw from the range of available views and to build a coherent view with the different elements.

The early Chinese thinkers were concerned about the inadequacy of language to capture the complexity and diversity of life and thought. Yet, they also realized that language was a powerful force in the society as it could be used as an instrument of political control. The Confucians were keen to incorporate language into their ethico-political agenda. In their theory of the rectification of names, they proposed that a normative use of titles (*zhengming*) will help to shape the behaviour of the people. The later Mohists and the Mingjia attempted to systematize the aspects of language. However, they were confounded by the mismatches between language and reality.

Correlative thinking is, perhaps, one of the best features of Chinese philosophy. One can find the key elements of correlative thinking in the celebrated work, the *Yijing* (*The Book of Changes*). Though it was used as a divination manual in the early ages, the later commentaries – its appendices – bring forth the sum and substance involved in Chinese philosophy. Aspects of correlative thinking permeated different spheres of life and it seems to make its appearance in different forms in the Chinese society even today. The appendices of the *Yijing* are a product of the world view that understands correlations between individual entities across different realms. They endorsed key aspects of Confucianism including the heightened role of the ruler, the providence of heaven and earth, the capacity of human beings to improve their situation and hope in a socio-political utopia wherein individual and social ends coincide. Chinese thought places emphasis on observations of the concrete, phenomenal world as the basis of reflection. Careful observation of one's world was prominent in the pre-Qin debates. The Confucian, Mohist, Daoist and Legalist questions about organizing the human world and the Daoist, Mohist and Mingjia preoccupations with language and its associations with reality are expressions of concern about how to deal with situations and vicissitudes in life. The solution to these questions in Chinese line of thinking requires observation and understanding of the natural, political and social environments as well as the relations between entities.

The tendency of Chinese philosophy to take a holistic perspective is articulated in different conceptions of the "whole". The early Confucians focused on human society, Mohists on a utilitarian concern for the benefit of all and Daoists in the overarching perspective of Dao. The *Yijing* similarly has a holistic focus and it describes how in terms of an encompassing whole the evolution of events and processes through time are comprehended enough.

There have been interesting and insightful studies of *li* and *ren* undertook by contemporary scholars of the West. Recently, a number of scholars have turned their attention to the concept *yi* (appropriateness) in the *Analects*. They argue that *yi* adds another layer to moral reasoning in Confucianism. Identified as "appropriateness" or "right", *yi* plays a particular role in practical deliberation as it reflects the Confucian concern for ethical appropriateness rather than normativity. That is, there is emphasis on doing the "right" thing in a particular context, rather than merely following a rule or norm. Comparative ethical analyses like these have immense benefits for philosophical inquiry and dialogue across different philosophical traditions. This, in fact, makes Chinese ethical philosophy unique. It makes philosophy in general and ethics in particular more and more pragmatic and applied. Especially in ethics and moral philosophy, scholars note that Confucian philosophy attends to the context of social engagement and focuses on moral practice in a much greater way than that of the traditional moral philosophical ways.

Other recent examples of productive encounters include the comparisons of Confucian *ren* and the feminist ethic of care, and discussions of environmental and ecological thinking in Chinese philosophies, etc.

Another contemporary rendition of *ren* and *li* is to emphasize their significance in self-cultivation in contemporary socio-political contexts. The interpretation of *ren* as "person-making" — though sometimes criticized as rather too post modern — has been influential in discussions of Confucian tradition in a democratic context. Another significant discussion in socio-political philosophy concerns the status of *ren* and *li* in the continuing development of culture and society in East Asian countries. A good example is the issue of the place and continuing significance of Confucian philosophy in a global context in which human rights are deemed fundamental.

The study of *ren* and *li* prompts further enquiry into issues associated with the moral cultivation of the self in a relational, socio-political context. One important issue concerns the concept of the self and relationality. In Confucian thought, the cultivation of mutually enriching relationships is integral to the self and its identity. This concept of an interdependent self generates a view of morality that defies normativity and generalization. It focuses on the practical realization of human goodness in lived contexts. Confucian philosophy highlights the need for moral philosophers to consider the concept of the interdependent self and how it is constituted by its relationality.

Whether Confucian philosophy engenders a collectivist ideology is a topic worthy of consideration. The collectivist point of view is contrasted with an individualist philosophy that is a defining characteristic of liberal democratic societies. A thorough understanding of Confucianism actually challenges the collectivist–individualist characterization of socio-political organizations. In fact, the Confucian concept of the interdependent self, which sits at the crossroads of *ren* and *li*, cannot simply be characterized as embodying a collectivist approach to socio-political organization. The cultivation of particular relationships is critical to be well behind of both society and the individual. In fact, Confucian philosophy offers a complex, realistic picture of self-in-community.

The above view of what is fundamental stands in stark contrast to those criteria in traditional Western moral philosophy including impartiality, objectivity and universality. Moral philosophers in the Western tradition are seem to be aware of the inadequacies of these criteria of morality as demonstrated in the vast literature. Nevertheless, one cannot simply abandon them because they are indeed integral to morality and moral reasoning. Perhaps the Daoist ethical considerations in *ziran-wu-wei* could enhance the application of these criteria. A dialogue between the two traditions could produce an ethics that is consistent and reliable, that also seeks to recognize and encourage spontaneity in human actions and decisions.

The comparative discussion about *ren* is important as it sheds light on a critical concept in Chinese philosophy. *Ren* plays a key role in Confucian philosophy, in articulating its picture of humanity and the good life. In Mohism, the role of *ren* is somewhat diminished though still a part of its theory of collective well-being. Both visions were optimistic in recommending moral guidance as one of the tasks of government. This accounts for why the Confucians and Mohists have sometimes been grouped together and their debate labelled Ru-Mo.

Mozi holds a list of social goods. For him, difference of opinion is to be eliminated by having only one standard, that which is set by the superior. The Mohist superior person is ultimately committed to social benefit and will implement a system of rewards and punishments to ensure the maximization of utility. There is little consideration for the welfare of individuals because it is assumed that collective welfare will also benefit the individual. The doctrine of Jianai requires not simply ambivalent non-violence but active assistance of others and concern for their welfare.

In course of time, many have tried to assimilate the traditional Chinese concepts and philosophical wisdom with those of the Western concepts. This is much evident in the three principles of Sun Yat-sen. The first principle, the Principle of Nationalism, which corresponds to Abraham Lincoln's idea of "a government *of the* people", maintains the equality of all ethnic groups in China proper and seeks equal national status for Chinese with all the people of the world. This doctrine urges all ethnic groups (mainly the Han, Hui [Chinese Muslims], Manchus, Mongolians and Tibetans) in China to unite as one nation so as to retrieve China's national self-confidence and revitalize its national creativity. According to Sun, his nationalism promoted eight kinds of national virtues: loyalty, fidelity, benevolence, love, honesty, justice, harmony and peace, all of which have their origin in

Chinese traditional culture but must be transformed to meet with the urgent needs of modern society. The second principle, the principle of People's Sovereignty, which corresponds to Lincoln's idea of *a government by the people*, holds that Chinese people must fight for their sovereignty through revolutions in order to set up a democratic government. According to Sun, Jean-Jacques Rousseau's idea that all men are born equal and people's sovereignty is given by nature are merely ideals or theoretical hypotheses found in classic political texts. Thus, Sun urged all Chinese to stand up for their rights and to fight for their freedom and equality by joining the course of revolution. Influenced by the meritocratic Confucian civil service system of traditional China, Sun urged that most of the executive offices of the government be assigned by way of examination, instead of election. This is to separate people's power from ability, so that people hold the power to govern while officials have the ability to serve (*quanneng qufen*). The third principle, the principle of People's Livelihood, which corresponds to Lincoln's idea of "a government *for* the people", claims to provide a middle course between capitalism and communism and to avoid either extreme by substituting the idea of "cooperative economy" for that of "the free market". Based on the principle of People's Livelihood, Sun argued for the adoption of two policies: (a) equalization of land ownership through taxation of property, and (b) restriction of private capital and expansion of state capital. Accordingly, the government should monopolize ownership and management of electricity, banking, mass transportation and so forth, and leave medium and small-sized businesses free room for their own development. Thus, the third principle takes people's livelihood in food, clothing, housing and transportation to be of primary importance and demands that government assume full responsibility for this. Above all, Sun proclaimed that his "Three Principles of the People" combined the choicest parts of Chinese and Western thinking with the Golden Mean (*zhongyong*) as a guideline derived from Chinese tradition. For example, the Principle of People's Sovereignty accepts the Western idea of democracy but denies its origination from "natural law"; as Sun observed, "all men are born unequal", and those born with more intelligence and capability should serve those less favoured by birth with compassion. To philosophers who demand scientific rigour and logical consistency, Sun's synthesis may not sound convincing and may seem to be largely based on personal observations and experience without theoretical justifications. However, from a historical perspective, Sun's "Three Principles" may be seen as a major effort at introducing Western democratic ideas into China. In this sense, Sun's attempt to combine Chinese tradition with Western modern thinking should be regarded as a typical example of the transformational trend in modern Chinese philosophy.

The true import of the traditional Chinese wisdom must be brought to the limelight. The contemporary relevance of the ethico-political considerations and the philosophical messages on personal excellence and social harmony of the ancient traditions like Confucianism and Daoism await further deliberations.

Bibliography

Primary Sources

Analects of Confucius. tr. Dim-cheuk Lau, Penguin Books, 1979.

Analects of Confucius: A Philosophical Translation, Ames Roger and Henry Rosemont Jr. (trs), 1998, New York: Ballantine Publishing.

Basic Writings of Han Fei Tzu, tr. Burton Watson, New York: Columbia University Press, 1964.

Book of Lieh Tzu, tr. Angus C. Graham, London: John Murray, 1960.

Chinese Classics with a Translation, Critical and Exegetical Notes, Prolegomena, and Copious Indexes, tr. James Legge, Taipai: SMC Publishing, 1893.

Ethical and Political Works of Mo Tzu, tr. Yi Pao Mei, London: Arthur Probsthain, 1929.

Lao Tzu and Taoism, tr. Kaltenmark, University Press, 1969.

Tao Te Ching, tr. J.J.L. Duyvendak, London: John Murray, 1954.

Tao Te Ching, tr. Chu-Ta-Kao, London: Unwin Paperbacks, 1972.

The Book of Mencius (see Mencius 2004).

Secondary Sources

Ahern, Dennis, 1980, "An Equivocation in Confucian Philosophy", *Journal of Chinese Philosophy*, 7: 175-86.

Antonio, Cua S., 1979, "Tasks of Confucian Ethics", *Journal of Chinese Philosophy*, 6: 55-67.

———, 1984, "Confucian Vision and Human Community", *Journal of Chinese Philosophy*, 11: 227-38.

———, 1996, "The Conceptual Framework of Confucian Ethical Thought", *Journal of Chinese Philosophy*, 23: 153-74.

———, 1996, "The Nature of Confucian, Ethical Tradition", *Journal of Chinese Philosophy*, 23: 133-51.

———, 1998, *Moral Vision and Tradition: Essays in Chinese Ethics*, Washington DC: Catholic University of America Press.

Boisvert, Raywind D., 1998, *John Dewey: Rethinking Our Time*, New York: New York University Press.

Brayan, W. van (ed.), 2020, *Routledge Studies in Contemporary Chinese Philosophy*, London: Routledge.

Capra, Fritjof, 2000, *The Tao of Physics*, Boston: Shambhala Publications.

Chan, Alan K.L. (tr.), 1999, "The Dao de Jing and Its Tradition", in *Daoism Handbook*, ed. Livia Kohn, Leiden: Brill Publications.

Cheng Chung, Ying, 1977, "Toward Constructing a Dialectics of Harmonization: Harmony and Conflict in Chinese Philosophy", *Journal of Chinese Philosophy*, 4: 209-45.

Ching, Julia, 1978, "Chineese Ethics and Kant", *Philosophy East and West*, 28(2): 161-72.

Confucius, 1991, *Analects: The Doctrine of the Mean*, vol. I, 3rd edn, Oxford: Oxford University Press.

Creel, Herlee G., 1949, *Confucius: The Man and the Myth,* New York: John Day.

———, 1953 , *Chinese Thought from Confucius to Mao Tse-Tung*, Chicago: Chicago University Press.

De Bary, William Theodore, 1991, *The Trouble with Confucianism,* Cambridge, MA: Harvard University Press.

De Bary, William Theodore and Weiming Tu (eds), 1998,

Confucianism and Human Rights, New York: Columbia University Press.

Defoort, Carine, 2001, "Of an Implicit Debate", *Philosophy East and West,* 51(3): 393-413.

Diané, Collinson and Robert Wilkinson, 1994, *Thirty-Five Oriental Philosophers*, London: Routledge.

Dubs, H. Homer (tr.), 1966, *Hsuntze: The Moulder of Ancient Confucians*, Taipei: Linking Publishing.

Fang, Thome H., 1981, *Chinese Philosophy: Its Spirit and Its Development,* 2nd edn, Taipei: Linking Publishing.

Fingarette, Herbert, 1972, *Confucius: The Secular as Sacred*, New York: Harper and Row.

Fung, Yu-Lan, 1947, *The Spirit of Chinese Philosophy*, tr. E.R. Hughes, London: Routledge and Kegan Paul.

von Glasenapp, Helmuth, 1954, *Kant und die Religionen des Osten*, Kitzingen-Main: Holzner Verlag.

Graham, Angus C., 1967, *The Background of the Mencian Theory of Human Nature,* Cambridge, MA: Hackett.

——— (tr.), 2001, *Chuang-tzŭ: The Inner Chapters*, Cambridge, MA: Hackett.

Hsun Tzu, 1963, *Basic Writings*, tr. Burton Watson, New York: Columbian University, Press.

Jiang, Qing, 2016, *A Confucian Constitutional Order: How China's Ancient Past Can Shape Its Political Future*, Princeton: The Princeton University Press.

Kaltenmark, Max (tr.), 1969, *Lao Tzu and Taoism*, Stanford: Stanford University Press.

Lai, L. Karyn, 2008, *An Introduction to Chinese Philosophy*, Cambridge, MA: Cambridge University Press.

Li, Hwui, 1911, *The Life of Husan Tsiang*, London: Kegan Paul.

Mei, Yi-Pao (tr.), 1929, *Ethical and Political Works of Mo Tzu*, London: Arthur Probsthain.

Mencius, D.C. Lau, 2004, *The Book of Mencius*, London: Penguin Books.

Rosemont Jr., Henry, 1999, *A Chinese Mirror*, Chicago, IL: Open Court.

Schwartz, Benjamin, 1985, *The World of Thought in Ancient China*, Cambridge, MA: Harvard University Press.

Shun, Kwong-loi, 1997, *Mencius and Early Chinese Thought*, Stanford: Starford University Press.

Simpkins, C. Alexander, 1999, *Simple Taoism*, Dublin: Newleaf.

Skaja, Henry G., 1948, "Li as a Primal Concept in Confucian Spiritual Humanism", in *Chinese Philosophy*, vol. 3, *Confucianism and Other Schools*, ed. Chang Chi Yun et al., pp. 47-71, Taiwan: Chinese Culture University Press.

Tomlin, E.W.F., 1952, *The Eastern Philosophers: An Introduction*, London: Hutchinson.

Tu, Weiming, 1968, "The Creative Tension between Jen and Li", *Philosophy East and West,* 16: 29-40.

Waley, Artur, 1942, *Journey to the West*, London: Allen and Unwin.

Watson, Burton (tr.), 1963, *Hsu Tzu: Basic Writings*, New York: Columbia University Press.

———, 1999, "The Great Han Historians", *Sources of Chinese Tradition: From Earliest Times to 1600*, 1: 367-74.

Yutang, Lin, 1959, *The Chinese Way of Life*, New York: World Publishing Company.

———, 1960, *The Import of Understanding*, New York: The World Publishing Company.

Zachner, R.C., 1959, *The Concise Encyclopedia of Living Faiths*, Boston: Beacon Press.

Index